The View from the White Rock

CHARLES LYTTON

Charles Harman Lytton

Copyright © 2012 by Charles Lytton

For information about permission to reproduce selections
from this book, write to:
Charles Lytton
mulberrymoonshine@gmail.com

ALSO BY CHARLES LYTTON

NEW RIVER:Bonnets, Apple Butter and Moonshine:
The Raising of a Fat Little Boy

The Cool Side of the Pillow

Book design by PenworthyLLC
Cover art adapted by Barbara Dersch
Photographs supplied by the author

ISBN: 09852732-1-6 EAN-13: 978-0-9852732-1-7

It is with great pleasure that I dedicate The View from the White Rock *to my particular friend Charles Price Shorter— most know him just as "Chuck." Long about 1960 or 1962, I was in the fifth grade. While running the well-drilling machine for Mr. Hubert Grissom, I looked up from my task and a very long shadow crawled across me. It was none other than Chuck Shorter. This was our first meeting.*

I was ever so happy to meet this new person. Up until this day, I was about the biggest person that I had ever met. There stood a fellow with a big inquisitive smile. He was big, too, at least as big as a right small mountain, and no more than one year older than me. A friendship began that very minute and has spanned almost 50 years.

I have found Chuck shorter to be a most willing partner in about every one of my youthful schemes and shenanigans. He is also a most dedicated father, a great farmer, and honest to a fault.

He is a most accomplished editor, too. He does adhere to Miss Hummel's rules of the English language, something that I occasionally lose sight of.

Here is to you Chuck! I think that you just might be a brother of mine. You know, one born to a different mother and a different father too. But somehow we are just kin.

CONTENTS

Eat, Drink and Be Wary

What's a Body To Do

Remembering Old Country Stores

The View from from
the White Rock

Foreword

Growing up in Southwestern Virginia makes me feel like I have a kinship with Charles Lytton. I, too, grew up near the New River (in a different county) and playing in and around creeks and on a farm. So his perspective on country life is similar to mine.

Writing books has created a community within a community where I met Charles. About two years ago, we were in Galax, Virginia, with Chapters Books at the Leaf and String Festival. The first thing that caught my attention was the title of his new book: *New River*. To my knowledge, I have never before seen a book with that title. Ah, someone that appreciates the natural wonder of Virginia. So I bought the book and loved every word. I loved it so much that I read it out loud to my husband. The recipes are wonderful.

The View from the White Rock brings more connections with Charles. He knows how much I love a white rock called Mount Airy Granite, but that is not what he is talking about in his new book. Mount Airy Granite is my subject.

Charles is talking about sitting on a white rock on the river bank; passing the time away in deep thought (or in very little thought depending on how you think). There is nothing more tranquil than sitting on a white rock on top of the mountain, on the creek bank, or on the river bank. Trust me! If you are stressed, just close your eyes and imagine taking your shoes off and soaking your feet in cool Blue Ridge Mountain water. That will lower your blood pressure as quick as an RC Cola and a moon pie.

The Blue Ridge Mountains, a section of the Appalachian Mountain range, are older than the Rockies, which means we have lots of mountains that have eroded away giving us exposed rocks with rolling hills. These rocks were formed more ten million years ago. They truly are older than dirt.

In 1933, Franklin Roosevelt signed the New Deal, which included a public works project called the Civilian Conservation Corps (CCC). The CCC boys constructed the Blue Ridge Parkway following the mountain tops from Waynesboro, Virginia, to Cherokee, North Carolina. There are many locations along "The Scenic" where one can stop and "Sit on a White Rock!" I call that therapy.

My favorite past time as a child was hunting crawdads in the creek in my grandmother's front yard. Give me a coffee can, a stick, a piece of bacon, a safety pin, and a piece of fodder twine and I'll go crawdad fishin'. Now what did I do with the thing when I caught it? Nothing. Just looked at it, put it back in the water, and caught another. So much fun! Wish I could do that today.

When remembering the Blue Ridge Mountains, I think about the blue hue and fog that covered the valleys daily. When I was growing up, we didn't see the sun until around 10 o'clock in the morning. If you live there you take it for granted, because it is a slow awakening.

These are the things that I have talked to Charles about when we happen to end up in the same location signing books. Anxiously I await his new projects. They bring back so many memories of life in the Blue Ridge. He is a pleasure to work with.

Karen J. Hall

Author

Once and Forever: The Story of Mount Airy Granite

Wythe County, Virginia (The Images of America Series)

The Blue Ridge Parkway and *Building the Blue Ridge Parkway (Vintage Postcard Series)*, both with FRIENDS of the Blue Ridge Parkway

Prologue

If you want to build a ship, don't drum up men to gather wood, divide the work and give orders. Instead, teach them to yearn for vast endless sea.

Antoine De Saint-Exupery (1900-1944)

I DO NOT KNOW WHERE I heard this the first time, but I do liken it to sitting on the White Rock. It is just plain strange how you do the same things your parents did. I think it is a subconscious thing or something. Just let me give you an example that is both funny and, well, real, too.

I can remember when I was a very young child, my father, Uncle Shorty, Uncle Nelson, Gilbert Hilton, Mod Snider and others met on the railroad tracks at the railroad gate near the White Rock. I think that there were a lot of reasons. First, there was the old Lytton homeplace down in May's Hollow. Possibly habit took the Lytton men back to one of the places where they'd played as children. The White Rock isn't too far from the railroad tracks and everyone loved and admired the Old Virginian Trains. Grand-daddy Ervin had worked for the Virginian Railroad, and when they were young, my father and his friends watched Granddaddy go up the mountain. Also, once upon a time the old car road ran through the hollow up near the present-day pond. Back in the day people walked along the railroad between Whitethorne and The Old Price Station. This was even commonplace in my own youth. But by the time I came along, most of this stuff was long since gone, except the Old White Rock itself. It has been there forever and will just keep on being there. And for some reason hard to explain to outsiders who did not grow up on River Ridge, the inhabitants are still drawn to the White Rock.

The White Rock is nothing real special. It is nothing more than a low cliff that hangs out over the New River. The cliff is no more than 35 feet above the water, but the view up and down the river is magnificent. You can see the fields on the farm downriver a mile or more away. Upriver you can see all the way to the horseshoe bend in the river. Pictures of this view in all four seasons ort to be on high-dollar calendars. Another thing: on the railroad side, you are eye-level with the train engineers.

I have taken many walks to the White Rock. We always had a very large garden in the river bottom just below it, so me and Daddy (sometimes I call him Elmer, which is his name) were always taking the horse-drawn wagon down over the hill to the railroad gate. There we very often stopped and ground-hitched the horse on the railroad right-of-way to graze on grass, tall weeds and honeysuckle. Old Fanny, that was the original horse, just loved grazing there.

"Just let her eat her fill. We ain't in no hurry at all," Daddy would say. "When her old belly is full, she just loves to plow corn."

Once Old Fanny had started to eat, we began to drift off to the Whiterock to just set in the spring sun and talk and maybe laugh at the stories told by other men who lived up and down the River Ridge. Sometimes others would join us. Sometimes they would already be there.

One of my favorite things was the trains. On the side opposite the river, the bank was about as high off of the railroad tracks as the train engineer. So when the trains came by, I could wave to the engineer and look right in the cab of the locomotive. Often Daddy and I would pitch freshly picked tomatoes, green peppers and apples to the waiting engineer. He would always blow the train's whistle for me, which made me feel like I was as big as a real, full-grown-up man.

As I sit here and start to think back, another thing comes to mind. Near the railroad gate, on the railroad side, there was always a jar of moonshine or a bottle of store-bought liquor of some kind. It was pushed back in the shade of a limestone outcrop. "You just never know when you are going get thirsty or need to treat a snake bite or something," Elmer, Shorty or Nelson would laugh and say. They always stopped there and had a little snort before starting the uphill climb toward

River Ridge. They most often had a Mason jar of cool, clear water freshly pumped out of the old Snider pump. The whiskey bottle just set there. To my knowledge no passerby ever bothered it. I am sure that everyone who knew about the hidden bottle stopped there too. When it got low, someone just replaced it with full one and pitched the empty over into the ditch. Recycling had not been invented. A small brushfire once revealed a ditch lined with hundreds of spent bottles.

Through the years, when the new road was made the rock that held the licker (Liquor's how you spell it, but licker's what we said.) bottle was pushed over into the ditch. During heavy rains, all the old pile of bottles and beer cans was washed down the ditch, through the big culvert and down into the New River. The old railroad gate is now gone, and the original path for some reason moved to the west side of the ditch. There is not much left except a large patch of wild mullin weeds and the White Rock itself.

Time has a way of changing things, but memories don't change. They just stick with a person. Like them mullins—they make the softest toilet paper of all the weeds. Daddy and all my uncles said that this was true, so it must be. As for me, well, I have picked lots of weeds in a particular time of need, but mullins are the best. They are real soft! Daddy said, "Years back, we all picked mullin seed stalks and pitched them over to the side of the path. They just took hold and grew. Now you don't have to go looking for a mullin weed." Even today, you don't have to go looking for a mullin. Me, I have been caught short and was pleased to have them.

A few weeks back, in October of 2011, my brother and his family from Indiana came to visit. My brother, Michael, was visiting at the same time from Bulgaria. He is a missionary over in Bulgaria, so he does not come to the United States very often. Everyone was here because Ruth Lytton, our mother, was in the last days of her life.

Mike asked me to ride down to the "Bus" with him. I explained that the "Bus" was no longer there. He just looked at me as if to say, "I bet the memories are still there." Oh how right he was! So we drove down over the hill, and we looked at the river, watched for deer on the rock bar and just said very few words. There are times when words are a very poor means of communication; so we both just kept our mouths shut out of respect for the past times we had enjoyed standing in this very spot.

Without a word, in a little while Michael starts up over the old path to the railroad. I just follow along. Neither one of us is talking, but we both know where we are going. When we get to the railroad there stands "The Woolf"—that is Melvin, our bother.

"Just thought that I would take a walk, and here is where my feet brought me," said Woolf. The Woolf has walked over the hill and down through May's Holler like in the past. We start to laugh, joke and share some of our earlier remembrances of our past walks to White Rock. Yes, we had just taken the same short walk we had taken many times before.

There we sat on the outermost rock. We looked upriver for a while, then we slowly let our eyes work down river toward Whitethorn. We took turns naming the fields on the Virginia Tech farm and places on the islands and reminding each other of all the great times we had experienced up and down the New River.

There was just a plain comfort in our meeting! I think little meetings like this reaffirm the meaning of family and blood. I heard one of the actors in the movie *The World's Fastest Indian* say that you could live more in five minutes on a fast motorcycle than some people lived in their whole life. That I do not know about. I never could ride a motorcycle; I just was afraid of them things or something. I reckon that I would just have to ask Rick Wall and Brother Woolf; they would know about such things. But I am sure that I lived a lot, too, in just one morning, sitting on an old, cold, lichen-covered rock, with my brothers watching the New River flow by.

Yes, the view from White Rock is kind of a family thing! Ifn' you get time out of your busy day-to-day life and you're anywhere near southwest Virginia, you owe it to yourself to go sit on White Rock! You won't come back the same person. You maybe could spend a whole lifetime up there one day.

Time After Time
on the River

There Is Just Something About the River

WELL, ONE FINE DAY, Daddy asked me to go to Whitethorn and paddle the wooden johnboat from the big boat landing back up to the White Rock and sink it. The river had been part of life for as long as I could remember. A big gigging event was in the works for Saturday night. I grabbed a boat paddle and ran right down the hardtop; I did not want to give Daddy the chance to change his mind. I ran all the way to the boat landing, never stopping once. It was not more than two miles. There was a time when I was more vigorous and not quite so rotund. I was just kind of round, but I could run to the river with the best of them.

It was very funny. I had been to that boat landing no less than a thousand times. I had been there with all my uncles and cousins. But, this was my first time to go by myself. I was probably eight or nine years old at the time. Everything around the boat landing was different somehow. It seemed like the Arsenal water pump—the "intake" as we called it—was louder than usual. It stood out in the water less than a half mile downriver. I could hear cars driving in the arsenal, too.

The cows on the Adams Farm were making noise. The big electrical power lines that powered the trains up the mountain had a rhythm in their hum. It seemed like all of the old men sitting around fishing were looking straight at me, as if to say, "That is Elmer's boy, ain't it? Wonder if he can even paddle the thing." Or, "I wonder if he even knows which way is upriver." I just knew what they were thinking.

I carefully untied the boat and pushed it into the water to let it slowly start drifting downriver. The river looked much larger and wider then than it looks today. I inched my bare feet across the boat through the slime and water, untied a flattened paint can from under the seat and carefully dipped the water out so as not to make too much noise and scare the fish. The boat quietly started to drift downstream past the old post office. I knew everyone was looking right at me. I carefully sat down and got real comfortable. I bent over and picked up the paddle and slowly started up river. I could see the swirls around the paddle's blade, and at the same time I could hear the water rush off it. After a pull or two on the paddle, the boat stopped dead in the water, ending its backward drift. Then, ever so slowly and quietly, it started taking me upstream an inch or two with each stroke of the paddle.

Why, I did not know of a person in the whole wide world with a more important job or greater responsibility, and here I was doing it. I had waited for a long time for this job to fall to me. Often bigger cousins did these important jobs. I was really careful not to take the paddle out of the water and never once did I change sides of the boat with that paddle. I wanted to showcase my paddling skills to everyone. You see, I had been practicing for this day all of my life, so that when the subject of my paddling the boat came up at Tom Long's Store, I would get a passing grade. If the subject did not come up on its own, I would certainly bring it up. Everyone needed to know that it was me that was paddling that boat.

As I gently moved up the river, I realized that I surely did like this river. The water was clear. I could see the rock ledges and the moss beds. I could see the deep rock bars. I chased the reflections from the trees that seemed to move away from me as I paddled toward them. Once in a while, I would see a large carp and lots of perch and red-eyes. I even saw a mud turtle swimming around a weed bed. I was so close I could have grabbed its tail. Why in the heck did I forget a fishing pole? Well, I settled back to paddling and took out a plug of Bull of the Woods chewing tobacco and made myself ready just to enjoy the ride.

The Red Bull's balls were swinging low and today mine were dropping down some too. When I got to the islands and the riffles, I moved to the north side of the river and stayed with the long, steady paddle strokes and before you know it I was past the fast water. I knew I had arrived! You see most people got out of the boat and pulled their boat up through the riffles, and here I had paddled through on my first try. Some other day I just might try the bigger riffle between the islands. What a day, what a day, few better have I seen or read about, what a day!

Dad and Shorty met me at White Rock, the place where the bus would be parked one day. When I turned the boat toward the black willow tree with the spring beside it, they did not say "come in easy" or "watch out for the rocks." I knew that they knew that I knew what to do and how to come to shore. Daddy just touched his foot to end of the boat, and asked if I had had any trouble.

"No, no trouble at all."

Shorty then said, "It is a damn shame that Arnold left the boat at Whitethorn. If he had not been so lazy, he would have paddled it back."

I just said, "It was no problem at all." I did not say it, but I would have paid Arnold or anyone to leave it at Whitethorn again. I thought the next time they could leave it at Fishin Run. Bell Springs would be even better. It may not sound like much to you, but I truly had been waiting for this day probably for eight or nine years or at least all of my life that I was aware of.

I did not know until a little later that when I took to running down the hard top to Whitethorn, Daddy and Shorty took to running over the hill and down the railroad tracks toward Whitethorn. Unknown to me as I paddled up the river, they had walked beside me almost all the way on the railroad. They never said a word about it. I guess they did not want to mess up my newly found confidence. I guess they wanted to enjoy my solo trip on the river. I reckon somewhere, years back, they too had taken a solo trip on the New River,

4

and I can bet they enjoyed their trip as much as I had.

Daddy and Shorty would often tell me about how the river was before the dam was built in the town of Radford. The river ran pretty much free back then. Just like me, the river just went where it wanted to; I know I sure did. When it rained, the river came up. In times of heavy rain, it flooded it banks. In late summer when it was really dry, the water level went way down. Hell, everyone knew this stuff. I even knew that flood control and electrical generation were why they built the dam. I was smart enough to know things. Hell, I was in the second or third grade, wasn't I? I guessed everybody must know it. As I got older, they would still talk about the river, but they truly were not meaning to teach me stuff. They were just reminding themselves of their youthful days spent just below White Rock. Most of the people and even some of the places had vanished before I was born. But I listened and learned of the people and places just like we were on a first-name basis.

I wanted all of the boat-paddling jobs that came along. And if my listening to these long-winded stories again and again might help, well so be it. Now here I am trying to remember these same stories and things and telling them to you. I guess that they were just doing to me what I am now trying to do to you.

They would tell me this stuff about the old house in the holler and how my great-grandparents lived there. At the time, all I could see were a few piles of rocks, a few burnt pieces of floor joist, an old set of bedsprings and a headboard marking the cistern. Today, there is just a depression in the ground where the old cistern once was.

Shorty and Daddy told about the time the road followed the river to Whitethorn. As we walked up the path from the railroad gate to the potato patch, they told me how this old path was once the main road. In the summer when the pond would go dry, they would take the two or three horses and their four milk cows to the river. They turned them loose to drink water and eat the grass and brush along the riverbank and railroad right-of-way. There was a lot of grass on the right-of-way then. The Virginian Railroad mowing crews kept it clean. You could catch up a few grasshoppers and fish, often catching supper while watering the livestock. You ran your trotlines, collected your catfish and re-baited the trotlines. It sounded like all they ever caught was the big ones. To hear them tell it, in their day catfish only came in large and extra large. If you grew bored of fishing you just went swimming. Sometimes you just got too busy to fish, especially if the Snider boys were out. One of my favorite stories was about laying trotlines, something that I would later master.

All of the men, I mean all of them, told this story in one way or another. Please keep in mind that I read a book once titled *The Past Has a Life of Its Own*. These are some of the stories that were good enough to take on a life of their own. I think that some of the trotline story may have slipped into my memories of the past from my father's and uncles' own past. Aw, you know what I mean.

Back to the story. All of the men talked about getting the trotlines out and then catching up the bait for them. Here is the part that I just can't grasp. Just above Whitethorn there are three islands. There is a shallow sand bar on the lower side of the first island the one on the arsenal side of the river. Three men would take a large seine, one man on each end and one in the middle, to help keep the seine on the river bottom. In a few passes they would catch enough small fish, not minnows, to bait the trotlines, including small channel cats (channel catfish) up to ¼ pound. The men would hold out their hand, palm up, and put the fingers on their wrist to indicating the size of catfish needed for bait. Sometimes they seined up fish big enough to take home and eat.

When I seined this area in the 70s, we might get a minnow bucket full of horny heads and shiner minnows, but no catfish. And very, very few of them were the length of your hand. Dad would say the little ones needed to stay on the sand bar to keep from being eaten by the big ones. By the 1970s both the big ones and the little ones were gone.

On the "L" Bridge

THIS ONE IS FOR YOU, Mike Long. For a few years, I did not pee on anything of any significance. On one particular day, when I got on the school bus I did not know it, but that primordial need to pee off of something was about to arise in me again. I was destined to pee from the "L" Bridge! I did not dream up this ritual. One young man (but older than me) on River Ridge told me that he had stood on one foot on the "L" Bridge and peed into the New River. I started not to mention my cousin Arnold's name here, since it might get back to someone, but I reckon it's ok. The poor old soul is dead now. I was a pall bearer at his funeral.

In Giles County, Virginia, there is a quiet sleepy little community of Eggleston. Back in the day this was a booming place with banks, warm springs, two or three stores and train stations on both sides of the New River. In fact, it was the first community in this area to build sidewalks. Yes, around the turn of the century up until about 1950 this was a bustling little community. But in 1969, there was little left. The school had closed, only one store was open and the little town was mostly empty buildings.

But, the "L" Bridge remained. It was a one-lane, shaky bridge over the New River and Norfolk and Western Railroad tracks. The bridge ended right in the little town itself.

It was a very warm day in either February or March. I was a senior at Blacksburg High School. Mr. Bill Brown was the baseball coach. He stopped me and one of my friends, Mike Long, in the hallway and said, "Mike, are you going to play baseball this spring?"

"Yes sir, I am," answered Mike.

"Did you drive your daddy's pickup truck to school today?" Coach asked. When Mike nodded, he continued: "Well, you need to get about two pickup loads of clay put down on the pitcher mound. Why don't you go on and get this done today? Take Charles with you to help. No one around here will miss him; why about everyone might even be glad he is gone."

So off we go!

We drove by my house, then his, and picked up shovels. We drove back to the roadside cut behind Mr. Sam Smith's and loaded up a real big load of clay and headed back to Blacksburg High School. We were finished in no more than an hour and a half. "We do not need to go back to school just yet," Mike said. I was in complete agreement. So we took the long way back to Sam Smith's.

We drove out Route 460 and back through Eggleston. I told Mike about the famous "Peeing off the "L" Bridge Ritual." He said that he had never heard about it, but he was game. We drove out on to the bridge and right where it made the turn to the left, we stopped the truck and got out. We both climbed up the bridge, which was no more than ten feet up and peed in the river standing on one foot. We got back in the truck laughing like all get out, drove over to the store and went in to get ourselves a celebratory Coke. The man behind the counter said, "I ought not to sell them Cokes to vulgar fools like you."

Well, we got our Cokes, then went and got the load of clay and made it into a pitcher mound. Then, since school was about over, we started toward home.

Arnold's ritual was right stupid. But, I reckon I was even more stupid for believing him and still more for peeing off the "L" Bridge. Hopefully tomorrow I will be some smarter and wiser. Today, as an adult, I just chuckle under my breath at some of the things young people do these days. Few have done the dumb things that I have done.

Never do I drive through Eggleston that I do not think kindly of Michael Long. He was a good friend and died awfully young. He might have been a little too easily led by my dumb thoughts. The old bridge is gone, too, but the memory of laughing like crazy at what we had just done still makes me chuckle.

Chuck Was Lucky

I DID NOT HAVE A GOOD Coleman lantern. Mine was one of those off-brand things with only one mantel. It did not put out much light, and to go cat-fishing in the proper fashion you needed at least one plug of Bull of the Woods, a carton or two of Blue Ribbon, a box of Winston cigarettes, a few cans of Vienna sausages, some saltine crackers and a good gas light. I had it all except the light. Without a light, you might fall down over the bank. You could not set back on your folding chair and watch your pole to see if you had bite. You could not find the proper food or drink in your cooler.

I caught up with Chuck at Terry Albert's garage and asked if I could borrow his Coleman lantern. He said yes, but that it had not been used for a while. Now, Chuck could pour anything into this lantern, and it would burn. I bet he could even have put cheap vinegar in it. My old clunker would only use that high-end Coleman fuel that came in one-gallon metal cans. You had to go all the way to Western Auto to get the stuff. But, I had plenty.

Well, I sat down out there in front of Terry's gas station, right where the old big oak tree once was, where the three roads meet. Chuck went in to work on a truck or wagon tire. I went to work on the Coleman lantern. The globe was just black, so I shined it up as clear as a crystal. I replaced the broken mantel while I was at it. I put it all back together and screwed it up tight. It was holding air pressure, so I released the pressure valve and filled it up with store-bought Coleman fuel, the kind that came from Western Auto, probably the first it had seen in a long time. I set to pumping it, and when the pressure was good I stuck a match in the lighting hole.

Rather than lighting, the thing exploded like a bomb. It was a very big explosion with a humongous burst of flame, though the fire only lasted for a few seconds. By the time the smoke cleared, everyone in the station was standing right beside me. I was still bent over the lantern. Not only were my eyebrows singed off, my hair was gone, too. There was nothing but little burnt stinking pieces up there. Everyone was laughing at me. Chuck said, "You may have ruined the thing with that store-bought gas."

When I got my eyesight back, I returned the lantern to Chuck. My old finicky one-mantel lantern was getting better all the time. I do not think that I was tough enough for a high-powered light like Chuck's. When I got into the truck I started to laugh too. When I looked in the mirror I saw my face was covered in black soot. The only clean places were behind my glasses. Yes, Chuck was lucky. Lucky he wasn't killed by that lantern.

Before There Was Global Warming

JUST A FEW DAYS AGO, I was asked about global warming. "What do you think, Mr. Lytton? It is real?" I had to scratch my head on this one. Being 60 years old as I am, I have these life experiences that I should be able to draw on. Also, I have been an Extension Agent for almost 30 years, and from a community perspective, I am supposed to know everything. Often, when a person gets to my door, she has done asked everyone else in the world and has made up her mind anyway.

I did what all good experts do: I answered a question with one. "Why are you asking me this question?" I asked.

Her turn. "For the past weeks, I've been reading a lot in the newspaper on the subject. It is all you hear on the news. How was it back when you were a kid?"

"The weather was truly different. I walked in snow up to my knees, and that is fact!" A soon as I said it I had to laugh.

"Why is that so funny?" she asked.

I answered, "My knees were about 10 inches above the ground."

I just had to stop and think back to my own experience and the old stories that have entertained me through the years. When I was a child, Uncle Lake told me about the times he and my Great Uncle Delmer would race the trains down the mountain on the frozen river. Uncle Delmer was my grandmother's younger brother, but he was just a few years older than Uncle Lake. Daddy said that Grandmother mostly raised him, so he was more like a brother than an uncle. Me, I can remember him, but by the time I was any size at all he had moved on toward Maryland, into what Uncle Shorty called "the land of spaghetti and sour wine."

In the early 1920s and 1930s, before the Claytor Dam was built, the New River froze over solid. "Solid as a silver dollar," Uncle Delmer would say. People living on the Flanigan Farm would drive horse-drawn wagons across the river loaded with grain to be ground at the Tom's Creek mill. If the iron-wheeled wagons cut grooves into the ice or if the ice developed large cracks, the driver just moved over to a new, more solid place. This went on all winter. By my birth, the Claytor Dam had been built, and since then the rise and fall of the river as electricity is generated prevents it from freezing for more than a few hours.

The best story and the one I sure wish that I could have witnessed was told by Uncle Lake himself! On real cold winter nights, a big fire would be built at the mouth of Tom's Creek, and boys and girls and men and women would gather for courting and skating. Sometimes as many as 10 or 20 people would come. Hot coffee and chocolate would be made on the fire. Fresh meat would be cooked, and all the ladies would bring pies and cookies. An old wagon would be brought and used as a table. Also, lots of strong moonshine would be there. After a while, the older people and young'uns would just wander off toward home leaving the night open for the young adults to get their courting done.

How did Lake, Delmer and others get to the skating party? They harnessed the horse, hitched him to the wagon, and down the old road they went. Uncle Lake said when the wagon got to the bottom of the holler, the big kids would jump out and race to the river carrying their skates over their shoulders. As fast as you could get the skates on, you started downriver carrying your shoes over your shoulder.

"We raced the wagon, raced a train coming off the mountain, raced each other. The only thing we had to look out for was the open spots or thin ice near the riffles near the Little Island," Uncle Lake remembered. "To my knowledge, I do not think that anyone ever fell in. And, of course, there was never any remembering of those that froze to death."

As he told it, they rode the wagon down the old road along the river through the moonlight. "We ate our fill, skated until our legs were give out, hugged up real close to the pretty girls and left when the boys

15

wanted to start fighting. On cold, moonlit nights, we would race upriver to the open water below the big riffle at Lovers Leap. That was more than a mile on the frozen river. You could smell wood smoke and just maybe see the reflection of another real big bonfire. Others were out drinking and courting, too. On these nights both the ice and the sky were blue, and the moon's reflections just kind of raced along with you.

"On the way home, we would crawl under a foot of old blankets and quilts, and the old horse just started back up the River Road. You could hear the mournful sounds of the ice as it moved and cracked. Some nights we would be out almost all night. It did not matter much, since we did not have any other place to go. When we got home, we would sleep a few hours, catch up on the farm work and head for Whitethorn again. As long as the snow wasn't deep and it was cold, we went to the river!"

Back to the original question about global warming. Today, we pump oil made out of dead dinosaurs out of the great state of Alaska. Once upon a time, a million or more years ago, it must have been warmer up there than it is today. But, it is warmer right here and right now than it was 60 years ago. So, to be real honest, I don't know.

People One Meets on the River Bank

As I ONCE STATED, every once in a while people just showed up for gigging. On one right pleasant late fall evening, we had a fire built up and all of us had had a cold beer or two, even me. The air temperature was well above freezing, but you still needed a coat on. Along with Uncle Shorty, Daddy, Chuck Shorter, Mod Snider and me, there was Russ Spock, the master gig maker from North Carolina who had come to check on the durability of his handcrafted gigs. It was not too late in the night, but everyone had taken a round or two gigging. Up walked Gilby Brown and John Dinker, both real close to knee-walking drunk.

Gilby announced that he was going gigging. I did not want to take him out, since he could hardly stand up. Plus, he was dressed more for a trip to the North Pole than for gigging. He had on a big old Army coat and a big pair of leather knee-boots. He was not going to get cold.

Gilby climbed into the front of the boat, and since I was at this point the number-one poler, I had to be the one taking him out for a round. One of the people on the bank pushed the boat off the shore. We had drifted out about 60 or 70 feet from the bank when I started turning the boat toward the arsenal bank. In the process Gilby fell over the front. Everyone on the bank was hollering to get Gilby out of the water before he drowned, so I ran to the front of the boat and grabbed hold of the gigging light wire, thinking that I would just pull him up. But, no, the crazy drunk man just turned loose. I could see him down there just kicking and thrashing. He wasn't more than 10 to 12 feet down. He could have just stood up and walked out if'n he wanted to. Then I realized that his big boots were full of water, and his coat had soaked up a lot of water too. So, I took my good boat pole and ran it between Gilby's legs. Using it like a lever, I prized him up off the bottom.

When he hit the surface and that cold air hit him, he took to shaking like a dog trying to pass a peach seed sideways. He sounded like a small thumper engine as he sucked in air for a minute or two. A thin fog rose up off him, too. He was freezing cold. For a while, he was the major cause of air pollution on the river, because of his really bad breath. By the time I got him to the bank, he was stone-cold sober and shaking like a leaf in a windstorm, and his teeth were chattering uncontrollably. He sat by the fire for a few minutes, announced that he was going home, and up the hill he walked. No one even went to check on him.

We kept on gigging and drinking beer and just about any kind of booze one could find. Elmer dragged out a new bottle of Kessler or something. Strong, nasty and cheap, those were Daddy's criteria for his booze.

As the evening progressed, we got less gigging done. "T-Bone" was standing down by the river holding a gig. He had gotten about as drunk as Old Gilby Brown was and started talking in some kind of different language. He might have been brushing up on his Martian, but you could not prove it by me, since I speak no Martian at all. He took to whirling and stumbling, and he started to fall with his gig in hand. Onlookers stepped back for their own safety; no one wanted to be stabbed by a sharp gig. He fell all the way up the riverbank with that gig still in his hand. When he passed through the crowd, not one soul moved to help him. Not one soul was sober enough to move much out of his way either. He fell under one of the old metal outside sleeping beds— clean up under it. The only comment from the crowd was: "He is good, ain't he?" Someone crawled under the bed and took the gig from him, and the gigging started over. T-Bone just stayed under the bed for a while.

That was the night that John Dinker said that a Vidalia onion was just as sweet as an apple. Russ Spock had brought a few with him. Anyway, John picked up one of the onions about the size of a small cantaloupe and set there until he ate it all. Everyone just watched in amazement as the onion juices ran down John's chin and his eyes watered. One of Mr. Dinker's nicknames was the "The Dirty Man." On a regular day, you could smell Mr. Dinker long before you could see him. You did not need a flashlight to know he was coming. There was no need to try; you simply could not hide from his aroma. After that big onion, he was truly ripe. Later that night everyone piled into the bus to go to sleep. In came John. He gave that old dirty black hat of his a throw, rolled back the covers on the bed Russ was sleeping in and crawled in. Russ said, "Oh my, oh my Lord, oh my help us all." He got out of there real quick; I don't know where he went. He just kind of vanished into the night and did not come back until morning.

The Community and the Cabin

THE TRUTH IS A DEAD ANIMAL did not have a chance along the river. This is how it all started. Wimpy Williams had an old ewe on the farm that he was going to have to get rid of, so a bunch of us decided that we would just barbeque that sheep. She was not a lamb; she was real old and real tough!

We hastily built a barbeque place near the cabin, complete with a smaller place for burning wood to make fresh wood coals for cooking. The old animal was killed and skinned and taken to the river where it hung in a tree waiting for tomorrow. We asked a man known for barbequing skills for assistance with a barbeque sauce. He had a salt, vinegar, red and black pepper, ketchup and brown sugar concoction that was great. I know that when this sauce boiled, it would clean out your sinus cavities all the way to your adenoids. Smelled bad; tasted good.

The next day, we set the ewe to cooking. We were good planners. We had built the barbeque pit within about 10 feet of the outside Johnnie house toilet. It was not a wooden Johnnie; it was an old telephone booth with a glass door. It never did burn down. Most of the men used it, while many of the ladies just crossed their legs real tight and held on. After dark, though, even they loosened up a bit and braved the path past the barbeque pit. Some would say to me, "When are you going to fix this outhouse up?" For me, at this time, it was already fixed up. I kept telling myself that, one of these days, I was going to make a brand new real wooden toilet, one that you do your business in and enjoy the peace and quiet. I never did. When no one was there, the telephone booth did give you a great view of the river and seemed to work just fine. It always kind of reminded me of the old toilet up at the house. There, I could set and watch the wildlife; here, I could watch the river.

It was a very warm spring day, with a warm night coming. Truly, life was great. That sheep took five or six hours to cook. We had told everyone we saw the day before to come and bring a dish of food. By the time the sheep came off the grill, more than 30 people were there. Everyone had a great time and had eaten some great food too. The best part was the people themselves. They covered the whole spectrum of local folks.

This cookout thing did not end there. For the next three or four years, if an animal took to limping, strayed close to the fence, was just too slow, or looked like it could be bought real cheap, it got itself roasted. The call for covered dishes of food went out, and people came. One night I think that more than 75 showed up.

Of course, we did do some drinking, too. One night I woke up in my bed, yes my bed, with Ham Hinkley and Lonnie Hinkley. No, they were not related.

Well, I soon found me a place to sleep on one of the orange couches. Some unknown person had started claiming it. I kind of moved in on her some, she moved over some, and there we were face to face and right close. The smell was much better than those in my bed; them other rascals were right strong.

Another time—and there is a picture somewhere to prove this one—Chuck had brought a few quart jars of white lightning. We must have sipped a lot of it, for there in the picture are Chuck, Melvin, and me lying on the ground just about passed out. The picture looks like dead outlaws lined up for an Old West photograph after a hanging. Only we weren't all the way dead yet; just mostly dead. It was Wednesday before I could go check on Chuck. He was no better. Not long ago Chuck said that he still has one quart of the stuff. He can just keep it.

When the meat was cooking, people on the river came close to the cabin just to see what smelled so good. They did not stop unless you knew them. There was a railroad track less than 200 feet from the back of the cabin. Trains at that time were very long, so long that to get over the mountain, it took engines on both the front and back of the train. Locals called the engines on the back "pushers." The pushers stayed in Whitethorn. They helped one train up the mountain and drifted back to Whitethorn to wait for the next one. We were barbequing an animal one time, and the drivers of the pusher stopped, so we sent each of them a plate of barbeque. Thereafter, the pusher always slowed down and blew his whistles at the cabin.

From Here
to Yonder
on River Ridge

I Once Had an Old 1964 Chevrolet Pickup Truck or Country Boys Do Take Care of One Another

IT WAS THE SUMMER OF 1969. I had just finished high school and was looking for some direction in this here life of mine. To help me look, I bought an old truck from Mr. Myers for $750. It was a well-cared-for, blue and white, half-ton Chevrolet pickup. I was at that time working at the Mick or Mack Grocery Store. I had spent my whole summer helping Daddy add two rooms and a bathroom onto the house and had spent all summer hunting, fishing and working. About the only other thing I had done was purchase a new shotgun: a 12-gauge Springfield with a 36-inch, full choke barrel and three-inch magnum chamber. If you shot a squirrel with it you had to be on the other ridge to keep from tearing up the squirrel so bad that all that would be left was feet. Good for duck hunting, though.

Come fall, I had money burning a hole in my pocket and at 18 years old I needed transportation. Well, like it was for all boys on River Ridge, that meant I needed and wanted a pickup truck. I looked at all the car lots in the area, and there was nothing that I could afford. I guess I could have used my $1,000 for a down payment on a new truck and borrowed the rest of the money, but I had heard Uncle Shorty and Nelson talk about the pitfalls of owing people and banks money and just did not want to go down that path. I had seen my father on that very path all of my life. So, I started to look for something I could afford. I thought, "I may not like it, but I can afford it and that's what is important."

Uncle Shorty told me one morning that Mr. Brogan Myers had bought a new Ford pickup truck and was thinking about selling his old blue and white one. He lived just a few miles up the road from the house on River Ridge, so Daddy and I drove up there and looked the 1964 Chevrolet over. From the second I saw it, I knew that I needed and wanted this truck. It was in great running order, and the engine sounded like new. So, I gave Mr. Myers $750 and drove the thing straight to Christiansburg and bought tags, then went over to the State Farm Office and purchased insurance. Next, Daddy and I drove the truck to a tire shop and purchased four brand new recapped tires for my truck. I was now broke as a convict and needed a job just to purchase a tank of gas. But, I still liked the blue pickup truck. I must be truthful here: the inside of the truck smelled just like one of those real big black cigars that Mr. Myers was always smoking. Over time I got used to the odor. I just started smoking cigars and cigarettes and chewing tobacco and dipping snuff in the truck. That made the smell more bearable, especially on rainy days when it smelled like Mr. Myers was setting right there in the truck smoking his big King Edward.

As luck would have it, I had found permanent work at the Mick or Mack Grocery Store in Blacksburg. I did not like it much, but bagging groceries and chopping lettuce kept me in cigarettes, beer and gas. As time passed, I got to know a lot of regular customers, salespeople and vendors. After a little more time had passed, I was responsible for restocking shelves with their merchandise. I kept the shelves for spices, soda pop, beer and wine full, clean and dusted.

This was good for store sales and good for the salesmen, since the more stock they sold, the more money they made. The same was true for the Mick or Mack Store. But, I did not do this for the store's good or the salesmen's benefit. No sir, I did it for the perks or samples the salesmen gave me. I always seemed to have a carton of beer or sometimes two setting on the seat of my truck. About every weekend, one of the salesmen would give me a case of pop. Around Thanksgiving and Christmas I found a small box of herbs and spices for my holiday meal. One time I found a canned ham. I took all of these things to River Ridge. Some went to Grisons' Cabin, some over to Chuck's Cabin, and some went home. One time I found two cases of Rolling Rock Beer in the back of my trusty blue truck. Chuck Shorter and I sure did treasure those little green bottles when we were spraying stick weeds a hot afternoon not much later. On the day before New Year's Eve in the winter of 1972, a lot of little jars and cans appeared in the back of my truck. That evening when I started home, I discovered two quarts of white moonshine liquor, one quart of J.W. Corn, a cheap bottle of Almondine Pink Chablis, and two or three cases of beer. "Yessir, it is going to be a great weekend, and I will be forever remembered as the life of the party." So I am thinking.

As it turned out, this just wasn't going to be! Just outside of Prices Fork on the way to River Ridge

I am driving along and see six or seven young men thumbing their way back to Wake Forest. I pull over to the side of the road and drive up in Melvin Overstreet's driveway a short ways; I tell them that some can ride up front and some can ride in back. The passenger door opens and the boys start piling in. I hear a loud hum of a car coming fast. The boys from Wake Forest waste no time jumping out. Within one or two seconds, Myrtle Redins drives her brand new Chevy Chevelle 396-cubic-inch engine across Melvin Overstreet's yard and into the back of my pretty little blue and white truck. Like Daddy would say, "Before a cat could lick his butt, people come from everywhere." I am escorted into a house. The young men from Wake Forest are gone into the evening like a flash. People ask me over and over again, "Are you all right? Are you ok?"

I answer, "I am just fine."

"How much have you been drinking?"

I later thought about this question, I guess because I was a Lytton from River Ridge I must be drinking

But, the truth is I am scared to death almost. If The Law finds all of the alcohol in the back of my truck, I am cooked. Not only am I still underage, but I have no sales receipts for any of it. I could lose my job, and so could those who had given me these New Year's gifts. With the white lightnin, I can lose my pretty little blue truck too.

The police arrive at the scene of the accident and I am asked no less than a million questions.

"Were you speeding?"

"No sir, I stopped to pick up a hitchhiker."

"Is the hitchhiker here?"

"Yessir, we were starting to get in, when we hear Mrs. Redins a-coming and we jumped for our life."

"Were you drinking alcohol?"

I swell up like a toad frog and answer, "No, sir." To my surprise and relief he just goes on asking other questions. I answer, but I am so relieved that I almost can't hear him asking questions. In the background I can hear Mrs. Redins screaming and crying.

"Oh, what will Mr. Redins do to me? This is the second time I have wrecked this car this year?"

Well, when everything was over. I received a ticket for illegally parking on the side of the road, and Mrs. Redins got no ticket for running into the back of my truck. To this day, I find this very entertaining. The police measured Mrs. Redins tire tracks in the yard and the skid marks on the road. I was parked in someone's driveway and a car drove across the yard and hit my truck and it was my fault. At times, the law is right blind or some people are just more lucky than others.

When the crowd cleared, my hitchhikers and I started toward River Ridge. When we got to Wake Forest, John Henry Beasley asked me, "Ain't you going to ask about all that booze of your'n?" You, know with all of the commotion I clean forgot about it. Well, John Henry continued, "When they took you into the house, we took the beer, wine, and white lightning out of your truck and carried it over the hill. We put it in Big Nose Price's horse water trough. I reckon you will have to get out real early tomorrow before anybody discovers what we have done."

All I could say was "Thank you!" Country boys try to take care of one another.

Mr. Buford Redins was mad as hell at me for stopping to pick up them hitchhikers. "Hell, boy you stopped just so Myrtle could run into you and tear up my car again."

It was a good learning experience for me. I learned that you can trust good old boys. I learned that sometimes you just should not pick up hitchhikers if there are other cars on the road. Even if you are pulled all the way off the road in someone's driveway, someone just might drive across the yard and up that driveway and hit your pickup truck! Lawyers are expensive, too. My end gate and fender were scratched and dented, but that Chevelle had one side torn up from the front bumper all the way to the back bumper. One of my hitchhikers thought the car had wrecked earlier in the day. "The side was already done tore up," he insisted. That I do not know. I just had myself a merry old New Year, and so did a few others.

How to Unload a Sow Hog

I AM SETTING AROUND at Mom's house the other day when an old friend came by to check in on Mom. We got to talking and telling some of the old stories. Here is one that I had forgotten until I heard the words "Whoa Motor." Out of nowhere, I am down on the bank of New River with about 10 friends of old.

The day starts off much like any other hot lazy day in the late summer. We are off on a trip to Floyd County in search of three things: moonshine, a half dozen good-size shoats, and a big, already-bred sow hog.

We—Daddy, Shorty, Nelson, Gilbert, Mace Graham and a few other men—would like to have a high quality, high octane drink of moonshine. All of us boys are just along for the ride. As for me, I have never been as far away as Floyd County, and I am really excited about the trip. Floyd County is world famous for its good homemade corn licker and not much else. We load up in Daddy's old blue Carryall, and two or three other people are in the front of Shorty's old green pickup. All of the men are licking their lips all of the way over.

We drive up to some place out on the side of a mountain. A bunch of people come out to the car and look at us. They just don't say much. About each window in this old house has the curtains pulled back and has a nose almost mashed on the window looking out. Some of the heads belong to boys and girls about my own age, while others look like grown people. As for me, I just don't like this place called Floyd.

The people were looking at me from every direction. Out from the corner of my eye, I see a grown man walking out of the woods toward the house. Elmer and Shorty get out of the van and walk to meet this strange man. They look at one another and work their heads up and down a few times, then Daddy hands him some money. Daddy gets back in the van, and we drive a short distance and stop. Out of nowhere a man walks up to the van and sets down four half gallons of fresh corn licker.

One of the jars is opened and passed around. Each man takes a long, steady drink. Then he passes the Mason jar to the next man. While they're doing this, they cough and their faces turn as red as beet pickles. There is one Coke in the car—the chaser, which is right quick-like opened and passed around just as the moonshine was. After the last man has had a drink of the Coke, the coughing stops as quickly as it started. Me and the remainder of the young boys in the car just marvel at these men and how well they can drink their moonshine. The strong ones pass the Coke on. One of them says, "I don't see no need to build a fire in your belly and turn around and put it out."

Not everyone agrees. You can tell by how fast they drank that Coke. Also, when we stopped to buy that one Coke, no Coke was bought for us boys. "We will get you one on the way home. Buy you one now, and you will piss all the way, and we ain't got time for that."

We drive up into another deep holler to a farm. You know what lives at this stop by the smell in the air. Now, I am a farm boy, and the smell of pigs and hogs does not bother me one bit. Here let's just say the hog poop is more than a little bit nose-tingling. When I say "Damn," Nelson tells me that is the smell of money and bacon on the foot. All I can say back is "Damned hard-earned money."

We work around the hog lot and pick out eight or ten pigs and shoats. There is one big old sow at the end of the lot. "She is going to have pigs" the owner says. "If she don't, just eat her."

That sounds good. So everybody grabs a-holt of this big sow, and she is hoisted up into a waiting crate in the back of Uncle Shorty's truck and down the road we go.

True to Daddy's word, we stop at a small store on the side of the road, and each young person gets a Coke. All of the men together buy just one Coke— another chaser. We load up and drive down the road about a mile and pull over to the side. The open half-gallon of moonshine is passed around again, along with the Coke. After the coughing and gagging stops, they all agree that moonshine is some of the best they ever tasted. "Best by far; you just cannot beat that Floyd County corn licker."

After a short while, we arrive at the Tommy Road. This is the road to, you guessed it, the Tommy Bottom. It is a one-lane gravel road with limestone outcroppings in a few places and very, very steep.

The most dangerous part about it is that it's just a few inches wider than the truck's tires. As you go down the road, there is nothing to catch you if you go off the side except the railroad a few hundred yards below. This group of not really drunk men who are not really sober either just start down the hill. They never slow down to see if a fisherman or someone is coming up the hill. Moonshine gives grown men a kind of intuition. You just know things—like no one is coming and the like. Shine teaches men things like there are no trains coming up the mountain and there are no pusher engines drifting down either. We just ride across the railroad without stopping to look.

The old hog lot has been empty since hogs were killed last Thanksgiving. The weeds are tall. There are millions of blackberry briers. The ragweeds are 10 feet tall, and there a lot of small locust trees to eat. Unloading the pigs and shoats is easy: you just grab hold of a pig or a shoat and set it over the fence. The pigs just take to the place, running like they are set on fire. They love the weeds and such. The old sow is a different story. She will not move. She has done made up her mind to stay on the pickup truck.

Well, Daddy has done had two or three good solid drinks of moonshine, and his understanding of things is getting more clear by the minute. He steps up in the pickup truck, takes off his 48-inch belt and wraps it around the sow's belly. Before anyone can do anything, the old sow jumps out of the truck. Daddy is holding onto his belt, and the sow heads down over the bank toward the river.

You cannot see the sow or Daddy. The tall weeds, briers and small locust trees are just wiggling and parting. The tops of the sticks look a lot like hands waving over your head. But Daddy is hanging on. Everyone knows exactly where to go to help, because he is screaming loudly, "Whoa Motor. Oh for the love of Mike, Whoa Motor!"

In about one minute the sow stops, and we catch up to Daddy. He is still holding onto the belt, saying "Whoa Motor" over and over. For a few seconds everyone just stands over him and laughs like that is the funniest thing they have ever heard. Daddy has briers, thorns and splinters stuck all over his fat belly, but he is laughing too.

The old hog is very tired and out of breath after dragging him through the brush. After she is walked back up the hill and released into the hog lot, everyone sets down and has a well-earned long drink of good Floyd County Corn Licker. "Elmer I guess you showed us, but don't you think that was just a little drastic? I just don't think that I am man enough to unload a hog that way." Then everyone starts to laugh again.

The three full bottles are hidden in the brush along the railroad right-of-way. You never know when one of the pigs might get out. We load up and head for home.

When Mom sees Daddy, she kind of laughs too. She lays him on the bed, belly side up. He looks like a real big, half-cut-open watermelon all stretched out. She takes a needle and starts on the splinters and thorns one at a time. Every once in while she has to dig deep, and it hurts Daddy. He screams out, "Whoa Motor, oh for the love of Mike, Whoa Motor!"

You Can Get Killed About Anywhere

IT HAS BEEN SNOWING off and on for more than two weeks. Schools have been out for so long that I think I may have forgotten my locker combination. Cabin fever is starting to set in. The snowplow man has been real good about keeping the road between the Radford Arsenal and McCoy open, but the ice on the road has been more than an inch thick. It is so slick and icy that is a challenge to walk and crawl to the mailbox each day without getting hurt.

Terry Albert and I have done just about wore out an old car hood sleigh-riding off of the big hill. I know that we have done rode down about every small locust tree and all the blackberry briers. I have the small sores on my body to prove it. It is time to do something less dangerous, and something that won't leave scars.

About dark, we decide that we will hitchhike to Blacksburg and go to the movies. Mom and Daddy have no objections. Hell, they just want me out of the house, and they do not care where as long as I am going to be gone for a long time!

We start off walking. There are very few cars going out during the daytime, and there are even fewer on this very cold starlit night. It is so bright the moonlight is being reflected off the ice on the road. Every once in a while, a puff of wind will pick up some snow and hurl it at me so fast that it stings my face when it hits me. I am thinking, "I damn sure hope a good John Wayne movie is playing at the Lyric Theater." I guess we have walked for more than 30 minutes and not one car has passed us. The walk to the movie is starting to look farther and longer all the time.

Out of nowhere, two very bright lights come up over the rise. Before we can even get our thumbs raised, the car rolls to a stop, the back door on the passenger side opens and someone says, "Get in." We jump in the car just to get warm. In less than three or four heartbeats, I am thinking, "Oh, what a mistake this ride is."

The driver is none other than Hammer Head Wingate. I thought he was still in jail. The man who told us to get in if we wanted a ride is Calvin Vandergrift. These two would be bad company for the old devil himself. Between them sets a more than half-drunk woman. I do not know who it is until she giggles and speaks. It is Gertrude Huffman; she is the woman who testified against Hammer Head at his last trial.

Hammer Head takes off like there is no ice on the road. He is going up River Ridge faster than I would drive in the middle of summer. He has one arm around Gertrude, and he is holding a 16-ounce Blue Ribbon Beer in the other and with the other he's driving. Now, if I counted right that makes him having three hands. Oh hell, I just set tight and hold onto the seat. Every once in a while the wind kicks up, the snow blows across the windshield, and for few seconds Hammer Head cannot see where we are going. Then somehow the wipers manage to clean off the windshield. Hammer Head, Calvin and Gertrude engage in a rousing chorus of "Hey, Hey, Little Snow Flake," and down the road we go.

We are moving down the Linkous stretch far too fast for a night like this. My mind is locked on the "S" curves near the Heath farm. Calvin says, "Hey, Hammer Head, that is the last beer we got. Pull over the first chance you get."

We just kind of drive in or better yet slide into Bevan's Store. We bolt out of the car, and within a few seconds are standing inside beside Frog Bevans. Hammer Head and Calvin purchase another 10 or 12 beers. "Hey, boys, get whatever you want and get in. We are headed to town."

"No, it is starting to get a little cold, and this is as far as we wanted to go any way," we say almost in unison.

The walk back to River Ridge was long and cold. We were walking right into the teeth of the wind. But for some reason the snow just did not sting as much, and the walk went much quicker. To tell you the truth, I do not know whether we ever got a second ride or whether we walked the whole five miles. I do think that if Hammer Head had stopped a second time, I would have jumped over the fence and took to running. I was scared from the second I got in that car.

I do not think that I was much smarter after this ride, but I'm damn sure I wasn't any dumber. Another thing, each and every time I hear the song about little snowflakes, I am taken back to setting on the back seat with slick roads and a crazy man just driving and singing, while I wondered if we would make the next small hill and the next turn in the road.

Come spring, Hammer Head was seen about the countryside. So I guess he lived through the night all right.

Damn, Them Old Trucks Would Run Like a Skeert Hant

THE YEAR MUST HAVE BEEN 1973. I was working on the farm at Whitethorn. This is the same farm that Virginia Tech now owns. Back in 1971, it was privately owned. It was a clear, warm, fall day, with not one cloud in the sky. That day's task was hauling more than 100 steers and heifers to market.

The livestock market is in Narrows, Virginia. From Whitethorn to the Narrows Market is about 75 miles roundtrip. Chuck Shorter will be driving his own stock truck. A friend from Price's Fork will be driving his farm truck, too. I am driving the old, once-wrecked Whitethorn Farm truck. They are pretty much equally matched old Chevrolet or GMC trucks. On this day, each will make three trips from the farm to the market in Narrows.

Before the sun comes up, all three trucks are well into the first trip. This is starting off to be one very long and very hard day. Breakfast is nothing more than an oatmeal cake and a cup of coffee. Lunch may not even happen. There just isn't time.

About 4:30 p.m., the last load is dropped at the market. We decide to meet at the closest liquor store, which is just across the bridge in Bluff City. When everyone gets to a meeting spot, we pool our money and walk in. We are smelling real strong and have a thin layer of cow shit from head to toe, so we get a right sharp look from other shoppers. But no one says anything. We go up and down the shelves looking at all the different liquors. No, we are not window-shopping. We are looking for the cheapest thing we can find. You see, I never did have more than two nickels in my pockets at one time. I am sure that I did not contribute much to this purchase.

The purchase was Chuck Shorter's decision to make. Chuck was the only person of legal age; I was still just 20 years old—you know, just old enough to die in the Army, but not quite old enough to vote or buy legal liquor. That made Chuck a solid 21 years old and as legal as the start of Trout Season at 12:00 noon on the first Saturday of April. Well, Chuck settles in on three quarts of 100-proof J.W. Corn. Out of the store he comes with three bottles and not one soda pop for chasers. "Spent it all" was all he said.

Each one of us got his quart, climbed back into his truck, started up the engine and cranked down the window. We pitched out the J.W. Corn's bottle cap, and the race for home started. I set my bottle between my legs so it would not spill. The more we nipped the faster them old cattle trucks went. One would pass the other going down the hills. The stronger truck would pass the others on the uphill grade. I do not remember any cars keeping up with us or passing us either. We boilt the oil in them old trucks. Supper you ask? Why no, we spent all our money at the liquor store.

We run back down through Poverty Creek on the one-lane gravel road. We pull in at the farm in Whitethorn and leave my old truck there. The last of my bottle and me climb into Chuck's truck, and we go

43

tearing off toward Prices Fork to make ready for a trip to Princeton, West Virginia. Chuck is going to haul a load of Christmas trees to Blacksburg.

It is right cool, and I am riding with my arm setting out on the mirror frame. Not far from Lonnie Kester's house, Chuck makes a little swerve to the right and the mirror hits a big maple tree on the road shoulder. The mirror is broken; somehow my arm is not, but it is badly stretched. I laugh and inform Chuck that I felt the gate latch on the back of the truck when the mirror hit the tree. We just keep going.

My arm was very sore for days. Even today, when the weather is just right, my right shoulder reminds me of the drive from Whitethorn to Prices Fork. Yes, them old trucks would run like a scared hant!

Country Boys Are Strong

Ever since I was young, when something big, heavy and dirty needed to be moved or grabbed a-holt to, I was sent for. I was never so happy in all my life as I was when Chuck Shorter came into the picture. Chuck is a big, raw-boned boy of Appalachian descent. That means he is of strong moral character, full of good will for everybody, and physically strong, too.

One day the call goes out for me and Chuck. Right off you should be thinking that something is real heavy or real big to be held onto. An old man named Surface Martin is moving from Whitethorn to Riner, Virginia. When we get there, the house is almost empty, except for this humongous freezer. This is no ordinary freezer; it is one of the old ones. I bet the thing is a good eight feet long. It has a compressor that is as big as a wheel barrow. Moving this thing is going to be real hard. Mr. Surface Martin assures us that the freezer is heavy, but empty. Ruby Martin, Surface Martin's wife, has locked the freezer shut so the door won't be damaged in transit. "Oh yes, it is empty; that is for sure," says Surface. Ruby then gets in a waiting truck and departs for Riner.

Now, there are three others standing around looking kind of sheepish. One in this group is Surface.

He is old and weak, and you know right up front he isn't going to be any help. He might hold a door or something, but he is best at staying out of the way. The other two are his sons, and they are only strong enough to lift a short Lucky Strike; why, they are too little and weak to lift one of them long Pall Malls. So it is Chuck and me and these weak three others.

I try lifting the freezer door and find it is locked. Surface does not have a key. The two weak brothers just shake their heads, look down at the floor and take to mumbling unintelligible words; well, I think they were words. I still do not know if they could speak proper American. Again, Surface says that his wife, Miss Ruby, locked it so the door would not blow open. As I look this job over, I see that there is no dolly or hand truck anywhere, and no one knows where we might find one. Up until this point in my life, I have never even thought about using one. Now to be right honest here, Chuck and I have never needed a dolly, because we are both of Appalachian descent. Up until this time, nothing we ever hooked onto did not move. Be reminded that this day ain't over yet.

We look this job over some more and decide that the only thing to do is lift the freezer up and simply walk through the two doors into the other room. Then we can change directions. I think with a little twisting we can make it to the living room, then keep on walking across the porch and up into the back of the waiting pickup truck.

It is going to be the strain of a lifetime, but we can do it. I hunker down under that compressor and feel for a hand holt. When I lift you can hear things in my body stretch and squeak. The veins in my forehead bulge out, and I am having trouble breathing. This thing is heavy! Somehow I lift my end, but how I do not honestly know. Chuck has his end up, too. As we stagger through the doors, the floors squeak.

We do not set it down, because I think that I cannot pick it up again. Across that sagging porch we walk and make it to the pickup truck. You can hear the truck springs take the weight. My hands, arms and back are kind of numb and asking me, "What in the world have you just made us do. What is in this freezer?" We drive to Riner as slow as we can go. We both know what is waiting on us. All the way over we talk about how heavy this freezer is. That compressor must be a giant to make this thing that heavy.

We get to Riner and back the truck up to the front porch. Miss Ruby Martin comes out and says she has been waiting for us. We go in and look at the place she wants the freezer. Again, this is going to be a one lift kind of operation. That is if I can get it up. I am as stiff as a poker. Ruby says, "Did anything melt on the way over?"

Chuck and I say, "What did you say?"

The freezer was full of frozen food. If I had known what was in that thing, I could never have found the strength to do what I did.

This was awful good training for what was to come over the years: big heat stoves put in places you could hardly walk into; pianos picked right up and walked out of houses; almost grown hogs grabbed onto for castration. The list goes on. Yes, I think that strong boys are grown out in the county. But few jobs have equaled lifting and moving a full deep freezer for Surface and Ruby Martin. I have never seen more sorry boys, either. I do think that when they were little they should have been taken out and dropped like an unwanted pup.

I Even Tried My Hand at Well Digging

WHEN I WAS IN THE FIFTH GRADE, Daddy and Mom farmed me out to Mr. Hubert Grissom to help out with the well-drilling machine. I made a whopping fifty cents an hour, but it seemed like a lot of money to me. It kept me in shoes and tobacco and cigarettes. My fifth grade teacher, Mrs. McNeil, sent a letter home to my parents suggesting that I study a little more and spend less time with the well driller. You see, I was not making very good grades, so school was not a high priority for me. Mrs McNeil said that I had failed the fifth grade, but she was going to place me in the sixth because I was "much too ornery and picked too much." One year was about all she thought she could take. I was on the verge of sending her to Saint Albans. Miss Hall was seen crying when she saw the list of sixth graders coming to her class. I do not think it was all because of me; there were some real mean girls in this class too.

Mr. Grissom had one of the old-timey well-drilling machines that had a one-ton drill bit. The machine picked up the drill bit about two feet and dropped it. Slowly, but surely, it would dig.

To start off with, the machine was mounted on the back of an old 1946 Ford, snub-nosed, tandem truck. This was no ordinary truck. It was a worn-out concrete mixer that Mr. Grissom had bought at auction 10 years earlier. The well-digging machine was so long that it would not fit on a normal truck frame, or on one with a conventional cab. It had to be a snub-nosed cab for the extra length. That meant that the engine was literally halfway into the cab of the truck. Even when the machine was in transport mode it was very tall. By today's standards, this thing was huge. It might take from one to six months to drill a well. Obviously this was not one of the newer systems used today. What made the process even slower was that we only worked at night and every Saturday and Sunday. I mean every Saturday and Sunday. Well-drilling was a part-time job. Well-digging went on every day, rain or shine.

The well-digger had been at a house in McCoy for more than five months when we hit water. So it was now time to move the giant of a thing to a new homesite in Blacksburg, which was no more than a 15-mile drive. My first job was to pump up each truck tire. You see, upon arrival at the drill site, we jacked the machine up clear off the ground, leveled it and then set the frame down on very big wooden blocks. While it was up on blocks, the tires would just go flat. I could pump with a very large bicycle pump for an hour just to bring one tire up to pressure. That meant it took me a couple of days just to get all ten tires up to 70 or 80 pounds of pressure. Sometimes Mr. Grissom would bring a small tank of compressed air, and that made my life much easier. If one of the tires had developed a dry-rot leak, I would have to wrestle the thing off of the truck so Hubert could take it to town and get it fixed.

Anyway, I had to keep the tires equally pumped and watch that they held pressure. You sure did not want a flat on that monster. Once everyone was satisfied that the tires were up and okay, the digging bit was swung up on the side of the machine and the well digger boom was lowered into place. It probably weighed at least a ton and rested right on top of the frame. Then we jacked up everything and removed the blocks. There were no safety devices anywhere, none. Once the thing was jacked up, I crawled under and pitched out the blocks. This was never a problem unless the truck was sitting on an incline where one side had to be elevated more than the other. Mr. Grissom did the crawling under then.

When the thing was setting on its own ten tires and none had blown out—a very positive sign—the next step was getting it to come to life. Keep in mind that this engine was never started between jobs. It would set for months. It never, *ever* had a drop of antifreeze in it. The radiator was just drained, so I would fill it with water before I took a little broom and wire brush to sweep off the engine and fill it with oil. The oil always looked like Mom's jar of blackstrap molasses and was about that thick, too. Daddy said, "If the old thing can manage to dig a trench through that oil and find the strength to start running, it will eventually melt down back into oil. If it doesn't run, it will just blow up." Hubert would come with five or six large six-volt batteries. They would put one in and crank until it died, put another one in and crank until it died. If it started, I would just set in the truck and keep the motor running. You never let it idle, because it would just die.

Once Hubert and Daddy were satisfied that it would run, we went to work on the brakes and minor repairs. I would pump the brake pedal and hold it, while Hubert bled the air out of the brake lines. After a while, the pedal would come off the floor an inch. "This is enough pedal to stop the SOB," Hubert would say. If the old truck was missing badly, Daddy might clean the sparkplugs and ignition points, or even put in a new set of ignition points. He and Mr. Grissom did not believe in new parts. They would root through the old wooden toolbox and find a better-looking sparkplug or make a sparkplug wire out of some old electrical wire.

Now the damn thing was ready to start again. And, if were you sure that you could get it running again, it was set aside until about daylight on Saturday. Let me give you a little more information on this monster. It had both manual steering and manual brakes. The steering wheel looked much like a wooden wheel from a covered wagon. Also there was only one seat, the driver's seat, and it was nothing more than a rough metal chair bolted to the frame. To get the truck to stop, you had to stand upright with all of your weight down on the brakes. Having a snub-nosed cab meant that the engine was right beside your knee. Inside the cab, the truck came equipped with a removable engine cover or hood. It was commonly called the "dog house." Mr. Grissom said his had been lost before he bought the truck. The driver was setting about even with the middle of the engine. This meant that all the road noise, exhaust fumes, engine heat and any oil leaking from the engine came right up in the cab with the driver. Yessir, she was a little cream puff.

You always moved the thing about daylight on a Saturday morning, because it might break down and need the whole weekend just to it start again. Another interesting fact about it was that it had never had a state vehicle inspection. It had no headlights, brake light or turn signals. A car traveling in front and back gave the turn signals and the one in the back showed the brake lights. It had not had an exhaust system in years and roared like long-lost lion.

Just as the sun came up on Saturday morning, Mr. Grissom jump-started the old truck, an event that caused the house lights around McCoy to come on, too. I guess maybe people understood this truck needed to be on the road before anyone else started for town to buy groceries. Well, anyway, it caught and started. Mr. Grissom was setting in the driver's seat kind of racing the engine a little. Daddy set the big wooden toolbox in the floor of the cab, and I jumped in. I wanted to ride this wild monster. I liked to hear the exhaust roar. Later I would wonder what was going through Daddy's head when he just shut the door of that truck. He eased the lead car out onto the road, and the well-digging machine followed.

As we departed McCoy, I bet you could hear us coming for a mile. We were on a long straight stretch headed for the Bob Price Hill. I thought this was fun, just setting on the toolbox being bounced around looking down at the road through the hole left by the absence of the dog house. Big flakes of rust and pieces of old mud daubers nests were being pitched into the cab. Mr. Grissom was talking to me, but I could not hear a word he said. I thought that I might need to go to lip reading school if I did much of this. My head just roared from the noise. When he finally got the machine up in higher gear and high range, it quieted down a little. I still could not make out too much of what he said, but could hear some if I worked at it.

53

When we started down the hill, we were going about 15 or maybe 20 miles per hour, plenty fast for this old wreck. Plenty fast! But I had not seen anything yet. I was in for the ride of my younger life. If had known, I might have been tempted to jump out!

As we started down the hill, the truck flew out of gear. Mr. Grissom was fighting the steering wheel and having trouble keeping the thing in the road. And we were gaining speed, too. The gears were grinding, as he fought desperately. At this time, any gear would have been a blessing. All of a sudden the truck went off of the hardtop, and he pulled it back. We veered into the gravel on the left and tore limbs from a purple catalpa tree that lived right at the start of the little back road to Wake Forest.

The small, one-lane bridge was no more than 100 feet ahead. I closed my eyes tight and didn't open them until we stopped. Somehow, and I do not know how, we went across the bridge, made the sharp right-hand turn and missed the big maple tree that stood right in the middle of the three-way intersection. The whole ride from the top to the bottom of the hill could not have taken more than 15 or 20 seconds, but it was a very long time. It seemed like about as long as I had been alive. The thing came to rest right near Mr. Galimore's Store.

Mr. Grissom said, "What in the hell is that odor?"

I said "Odor, hell, I am setting in that."

"Boy you need to go somewhere and shake your britches."

"When we almost hit the tree, I closed my eyes and held onto the toolbox. When we hit the bridge, I wanted them tools in front of me."

"I closed my eyes too, but I did it when the thing flew out of gear."

"When we got to that little jump and started over the bridge, I think that is when I shit my britches, but it happened so fast I can't remember."

He agreed with me about that timing, then he said, "Remind me to put grease in the transmission before the next trip."

Daddy and Shorty pulled up beside us. "What in the hell happened? One minute you are coming down the hill; the next minute you are about to run over me," asked Daddy.

Mr. Grisson explained about the truck flying out of gear and how he could not get it back in a gear and the manual brakes would not slow down the machine. "And Harmie shit his britches," he added.

"Hell, I shit mine, too, when the front tires came off the ground there at the bridge. I don't know how in the hell you got that thing across the bridge?" said Uncle Shorty.

Well, we spent a few minutes checking the tires and pulling the tree limbs from the digging machine. "It still has water, oil and gas. We need to get this thing moving," the men agreed.

When we started up the hill out of Long Shop, it was very, very noisy. We were back into low gear long before we got to Tommy Pendleton's house. By the time we got to Gilbert Hilton's house, the thing was going about as fast I could walk. You almost had to set a rock on the ground to see if we were even moving. But, the old truck just kept on coming and screaming like a wild cat. A very fine mist of oil filled the air and rust pieces and mud dauber nest still jumped of the engine. Once we passed Sam Smith's, it was a clear ride all the way to Mount Tabor. By the time we arrived, the old truck was running pretty well and would idle independently.

Yes, there was some shit. I think that I was far too scared to do too much else. But, by the fifth grade I had already added a number of do-not-repeat activities to my life's list. One lesson was not to ride that damn well-drilling machine ever again, or my life's list would be a mighty short one. As an afterthought, put some grease in the transmission.

When we got the thing back up on blocks, I put many cans of gear oil in the transmission and in the rear end. Chances are good that neither one had ever been checked before. Ever! By the way, I did pretty well in the sixth grade. I was just taking a little time out of learning to explore making a living as a well-driller.

Dianna's First Airplane Ride and Maybe My Last

IT IS THE WINTER OF 1988, and Dianna is eight years old. Me, I am nowhere near as old and wise as I am going to get to be in the next three hours. It is one of those late winter days when everyone starts to get the cabin fever. Dianna and I had it bad, so for some reason we go for a walk—not your regular walk, mind you. We start walking across the VPI Campus and end up at the VPI Airport. (Just a few years ago VPI changed its name to Virginia Tech.) The air is just above freezing, there is some snow on the ground, and puddles still have ice in them. On their north sides the hills are still covered with an inch or two of snow. The south sides are clean and free of snow.

As we walk past the airport, we discover a big hole in the fence, so we just start walking down the runway. We look and see one airplane and then another. Then we come up on a man and his wife sweeping the snow off of their airplane. I hear the woman say she is not going for a ride today: "It is just too cold to go for a ride. Besides the damn thing does not have a heater, and we would freeze to death."

To knock the ice off, every once in a while the man gives the airplane wing a right hard rap with a broom. Yes, I said a broom, one like you sweep the floor with. I guess I always thought that de-icing was done in a hangar, or there was some chemical that one sprayed on the plane. We walk over. I do not catch their names.

The woman says, "Why don't you take that little girl for a ride? She looks like she wants to go."

He looks at me and informs me that he just needs to shake the oil up in the airplane. "I might just run up to Wintergreen or head west toward Snowshoe and see if anyone is still skiing. Your little girl sure wants to go."

I am still trying get beyond "Huh and well—well a. . . ." when we check the oil and try to see if there is any water or ice in the gas. By now Dianna is up in the plane. The gas looks clear to me. The owner climbs in and starts to crank the engine, and the airplane will not start. In fact, it will just barely turn over. Just about the time I think the dead battery is going to save me, the rascal starts up. I still do not know who this man is!

The plane sets still and idles, while he does the final safety check. I think he sees that I am a little concerned, so he does a second safety check. I slowly crawl in. Dianna has been in the airplane for the last ten or so minutes looking at tools, checking out a used carburetor, and other extra engine parts. The man jumps in, snaps a few tie-downs over the toolbox and the parts, hands me a large handful of rags and points to the door. He tells me: "Work them in the hole in the door and stick some in the cracks around it." I am setting in the right front seat, and Dianna is setting on the toolbox in the back. The pilot has a real nice, thick, hairy coat and a thick pair of gloves. He is ready to fly up to the North Pole, and see if Richard Byrd is around or something.

Now, I have got on a real good pair of low-cut, regular tennis shoes and an okay kind of coat, but no gloves. Dianna is dressed more poorly than I am. Somebody, whoever he is, mashes down the gas pedal, and down the runway we go. The little airplane doesn't take off; it just jumps up in the air. It is very cold and loud. The worst part is the plane is shaking like a constipated dog trying to pass a peach pit, and I am no better. I am thinking that some of the ice is still stuck on the airplane or something, and it is shaking trying to get the ice loose. The pilot screams back to Dianna: "Well, where do you want to go first?"

She get up. walks forward and screams in his ear that she wants to see her school, her house in McCoy and her pony.

We make it to Prices Fork Elementary in about a minute and fly a tight circle around the building. I am getting cold. My breath is thick and white, but the wind is whizzing through the airplane and will not let my breath stick on the windshield. It is blown away. We start for McCoy; we get to the house and look things over. Dianna points out her pony. The airplane driver—by now I don't think he is a pilot at all—turns the plane in real tight circles again. As centrifugal force pitches my body to the right and down, my right eye is stuck on the window, while Dianna has her face smudged right up on another part of window. She is screaming like a wild cat. I think she is going to die of fright. But, no, she is just screaming like she is riding a roller coaster and is having the time of her life. I am the one about to pass out. When the plane levels off,

I think we are heading for Blacksburg. I have done enjoyed about all my body can stand; surely the oil is shook up enough by now.

We get about to Prices Fork, when the pilot again asks Dianna if she wants to go to Pipestem State Park and check out who is skiing. In that instant the plane pitches to the north. I am holding to my seat while Dianna rolls off the toolbox. I am so very happy that the toolbox is tied down. I am about one quarter sick, and Dianna is having the ride of her life. I am just about to freeze to death. I sure wish that I had a real thick coat like the pilot; those big gloves would not hurt any, either. As we go over each ridge the plane drops a few feet. I can feel my stomach jump in my ribs. We are a little too high for jumping out, but not that much. I just might try it on the next mountaintop. If I thought that I could grab the top of one of those big oaks I just might try; this is no fun at all.

I am about as cold as I was the time we were deer hunting on Bill Williams' property when the fog froze on everything and wind blew down off of Mountain Lake. Dianna's nose is as red as a beet pickle and kind of swollen up like a light bulb right on the end. I have old rags stuffed in the door to keep some of the wind out. Oh, by the way, the man's wife is right—there is no heater at all. I pull off my coat and stuff Dianna into it. Finally, we make it to Pipestem. There are people skiing, but not many. It is too cold for skiing. We are so close to them that possibly they think we are going to land or chop them with the propeller. Everyone looks up and waves at us, then they are just gone. I hope they are all in the nice warm snack bar. Anyway, I am truly about to freeze up and break in two. About all I can think of is that song about the men dying of thirst, and all they can think about is Cool, Cool Water. All I can think about is heat and a lot of it. The very thin layer of mush ice is growing thicker in my eyes.

The pilot asks me if I have ever flown an airplane. I answer, "No, and I don't want to start either." The only thing that keeps me from freezing to death is my growing sickness. For some reason the pilot climbs up to about 4,500 feet and levels off. He looks at me and says, "Have you ever flown over Mountain Lake?"

I answer, "No, I haven't, and I really don't need to either."

Well, the motor kind of angles up a little more, and in just a jiffy we go over Mountain Lake. The little airplane drops down to the water's surface, and the driver—he is no pilot—lowers the tires to within a few feet of the water. Then he pulls back on the stick and the plane goes skyward again.

I am not keeping an eye on Dianna at all. There ain't anywhere she can go, except maybe she could fall out the hole in the door. But I have my foot stuck in that. Well, I think I do. I have not had any knowledge of even still having a foot or leg since we left Prices Fork. Mountain Lake is covered in a white layer of snow. When we go over the top and cross to the other side, there is no snow and the airplane jumps up a few feet. Then we drop down about 1,000 feet. My stomach is stuck down toward my butt for a little while. I am truly giving some thought to being real sick. No, not regular sick; I mean real bad sick.

Somehow I manage to look over my shoulder to check on Dianna, and she has her face stuck way down in the barf bag. The sides are blowing out then sucking in. I think she must have puked upwards of three or four gallons, maybe more. She sees the look on my face and walks up and climbs on my lap. She hands me the barf bag. Now my stomach takes to reeling and pitching. She screams in my ear, "I was only blowing up the bag in case someone needed it. You looked like you wanted it." The only thing that saves me is the sight of the VPI Airport just ahead.

When the airplane lands, my feet are truly numb and my legs are not working very well, I am cold to the bone and want to just go somewhere real private and ditch my cookies and maybe cry, too. I grab Dianna with my frozen hand and start limping off toward the hole in the fence. I never look back out of fear. I fear that Dianna would want go to the North Pole, or hell who knows, she and this pilot man, whose name I still do not know, might just want to go over the North Pole and on to Russia. I am just not man enough for any more flying.

In the Bible there was fellow called Lot, and God told him not to look back when he left Gomorrah or something bad would happen. This was the kind of exit we made: stiff-legged, lips trembling, but my good thawed out eye was fixed on the hole in the fence! The frozen eye just had to follow. I wanted to get away from this airport. I was sick for a week. By the time we were walking past the VPI football field, I could say words without my lips trembling.

I am not the sharpest tool in the shed, but I now know never to get in an airplane with a person I do not know, especially with someone with only a learner's permit for flying. Also, if someone ever hands you a bunch of rags and tells you to stuff them in the hole around door, jump out. It might be the man with the learner's permit, and he just wants to skeer the pants off you.

To this day I still do not know who the owner of that airplane was. I do not want to know who he is. Even now, I almost never drive down the road past the VPI Airport, and I have never walked back there again.

Driving by Memory

I ONLY TRIED TO DRIVE by memory one time. I learned my lesson. As it happened, I was about 19 years old. I was working at the Mick-or-Mack Grocery Store in Blacksburg. Earlier in the summer, I had bought a 1964 Chevrolet car from Mr. Joe Shorter. It was one fine car, with a sweet-running 283-cubic-inch engine. In fact, it was the first car I ever had. The only problem there ever was with that car was the heater. It was awful slow to warm up.

It is the last Thursday before Christmas. Each Thursday morning the Domino Grocery delivery truck came to Mick or Mack Grocery Store. Believe it or not the delivery truck arrived at 4:00 a.m. or a little earlier. Friday and Saturday were normally the two busiest days of the week. Because Christmas is just around the corner, this is going to our biggest sale week of the year. So on this Thursday morning everyone is scheduled to arrive no later than 4:00 a.m. to unload the truck and start restocking shelves. It is three days before Christmas. I remember this morning like it was yesterday.

When I come out of the house about 3:30 a.m., the stars are real bright, but it is cold as a. . . well a witch's uh, uh. . .broom. It is cold anyway. The frost is very thick on the windshield. I crawl in the car, and after a growl or two that wonderful 283 engine starts up. It runs right rough for a second or two, then settles down and sounds good. While I am listening to that engine purr, I start looking for an ice scraper. I find my little M and M Garage scraper and start on the windshield. The little thing breaks, and I give it a pitch over the hill.

I settle down in the car thinking that it will warm up soon. After a few minutes, I give up on the heater and start thinking that there will not be any cars at all this time of morning. So why don't I just start up the road real slow, driving by memory. The car will warm up more quickly if it is moving. Up the road I go. If I hear the gravel sounds on the right, I know that I need to move a little to the left. If the sound is on the left, I need to move back to the right to get back in the road.

I pass by Mason Williams' Barber Shop. I can see the big dusk-to-dawn light shining through the ice. The car is still cold, and ice on the windshield is as thick as ever. I can feel the ice on my mustache, too. I keep crawling up the road. The farther I go, the more chicken I become. Driving by memory is about the most stupid think I can think of. I really lose my nerve. I stop the car. I look around again for a scraper and find a piece of an old plastic cigarette case. I step out of the car to have another go at the windshield, but rather than scrape off ice, I fall over the bank and roll all the way to the barbed wire fence. The car is less than six inches from running over the bank! I manage to crawl back up the bank and get into the car.

I set real still and wait for the heater to warm

up. After I get going again, I am still just shaking. I drive to town with the heater running full blast. On the way home, I stop at Windle McCoy's Garage and have a new thermostat put in that great little 283 engine. It costs me a few dollars, and the car does warm up much better. I also pick up a half a dozen ice scrapers. The worst part of the trip is the small locust thorns and the briers and having to ask Mom to dig them out of my back and butt.

Just a few days later, a very small snowstorm passed over River Ridge. Before I left the house, every window was scraped off, and I swept the snow off the top of the car. I even took the broom to the hood. For some reason, and I do not know why, I do not even like for snow to blow up on the windshield and limit my visibility. I guess it is because I failed so miserably at driving by memory.

I told Daddy and Shorty about this learning experience. They had a good laugh; heck, everyone did. They told me of a man that once lived in Vought Holler. He had bought an older used car, one of the real old ones, something like a T-Model or a Model A that came along about this time. It had no heater at all, according to the givers of all information. This old man could not drive by memory either. He drove with his head out the window, and he came very near to freezing to death.

So the old man took care of this situation. He took a glasscutter and made a hole about the size of a walnut in the windshield. When it was real frosty or when the ice was thick, he could lean forward over the steering wheel and see the road through that little hole. The new thermostat worked just fine for me.

Today, at age 60, I have about every shape, size, color and manner of ice scraper. If any of the local garages need a few, I have plenty to share.

Getting Stopped by the Police

AT THE TIME, I WAS probably 15 or 16 years old. Yes, that is about right, because you could buy beer anywhere when you were 17. The story starts off at the log cabin in Chuck Shorter's creek bottom. We are setting around talking about making a beer run. For the life of me, I cannot remember who all was there. I know that I was, because I am the one doing the writing here. There was me, Jerry Noonkester, Chuck, John Toth and possibly Ricky Wall and maybe Jimmy Bland, too. Bobby Hill was not, because if he had been there, we would not have had to make a beer run. Bobby just always seemed to have plenty of Budweiser. Come to think of it, Bobby always had lot of beer period. He was real good like that.

Anyway, it has been decided that a beer run will be made. The only details left are: Where to go? What to buy? How much money do we have? How are we going to get there? Most important, who is going to go in and buy the beer? We are all big for our ages, but we are all still well under legal age. Yes, the devil is in the details, and planning ain't it.

We could go to Cecil's beer joint. I had driven the VW bus over there the other day during school. It was a short ride across town. I got me a hamburger and a beer for lunch. We could go to the tavern in Blacksburg; that's where a lot of college students buy beer. Someone knew someone at the beer joint over at Flat Top. How about Bevins'? Far too close, someone said. Jerry Noonkester said that he knew someone working at the Golden Gobbler Tavern.

You see, there were not many places to buy beer in 1967. The grocery stores were just starting to carry beer, but they were prone to check identifications and birth dates. What we needed was a place where the only two requirements were: (1) you had the cash money; and (2) you were tall enough to put the money on the counter. The Golden Gobbler it would be.

We put our money together and gave it to Jerry. He was given the task of driving to the Golden Gobbler and buying all the beer that we could afford. I was thinking we could get two or more cases. I wanted to go, too. So off we went.

When we get to the beer joint Jerry goes in and makes the purchase. I stay in the car for a few minutes like he asks me to. He comes to the door and motions for me to join him. I go running in as fast as fat little legs will carry me. There on a table sets seven cases of Black Label Beer. It is even cold; I mean right out of the cooler in the back. We load the beer onto the back seat of his old Buick and take off for the creek. Hello, Mabel!

We are driving through the VPI Campus. (Virginia Tech was VPI back then. Confusing isn't it? I am 50-some years old, and it still confuses the hell out of me.) Back to the story. The flashing lights of a police car come on right behind us. I do not know what to do. All I can think about is going to jail or being sent to the stone-cutting quarry in the Roanoke Valley and being forced to load them big rocks to make more of the VPI Buildings. Here come two very large flashlights, one up each side of the car. Jerry unwinds the window, and Floyd Noonkester sticks his head in the window. "You bunch of little shitheads. I have told you not to come to town drunk."

Jerry says, "Daddy, we have not drunk any of the beer yet."

"Well, make sure you don't, and go straight to that cabin or bus or wherever you all are headed." Floyd then looks right at me, "How is Elmer and your mother? I have not seen them in awhile."

"They are fine," is all I can say.

Floyd was a police officer for VPI at the time; he is also Jerry's' father. We could hear Luther Harrell (he was the other police officer) just roaring and laughing at us. I bet they were laughing more at me than Jerry. Jerry seemed right calm and collected. Me, I could have crapped in my undershorts if I'd been wearing any. I am darn sure they talked about the funny look on my face.

As soon as we hit the town limits, we cracked open two good cool Black Labels, and visions of Mabel flashed before my eyes. The only downside was some of the cases were beer bottles, and we were once upon a time going to build a pop-top chain all the way to the road. This week we did not add much more than a random link or two. Maybe we could get back on the chain next weekend we agreed. A mile or more of pop-tops ain't that many. But for now we all thought that it was time to go visit Mabel!

I do not rightly know what to tell you about what I learned from this experience, other than to go to Floyd's Store the next morning and get me an RC Cola and a BC headache power. Floyd would have them setting out on the counter for us after one of these learning experiences. I guess I learned that most all Appalachian boys go through this phase trying to get to be young men. All Appalachian men know the growth phase we boys are caught in. And I guess I was doing as I had been programmed to do. I also learned a hard lesson when I was much older— truly the good die far too young! Both Floyd and Jerry were great people. Jerry never bothered a soul in this whole world and died before he was 40, not from alcohol either. He was a church-going man and could sing like a bird. He just up and died, and he is still missed to this day.

The Old Wooden Wagon

ONE OF MY FONDEST and earliest memories of River Ridge is of me setting in an old four-wheel horse-drawn wagon. I am guessing I first saw the wagon about 1955 or 1956, which would make me about four or five years old. By this time, almost everything from the past years had been replaced by newer and fancier things. On the hill (that's OUR hill), my father and his brothers liked a little bit of the past hanging around them. I think it reminded them of their earlier life, kind of like it is doing to me now. I think you know what I mean. The old horse-drawn wagon was one example.

This was a simple two-horse wagon used to pull loads of potatoes, apples, firewood and other stuff from out of the holler. Uncle Shorty and Daddy would haul loads of ear corn from both the river bottom where the bus would someday set and the Tommy Bottom.

In my father's and uncles' day, throughout the year the old wagon was often driven along the railroad between Whitethorn and the White Rock. The horses walked right slow, while all family members picked up lumps of coal that had either fallen or had been pushed from the Virginian coal trains. You got it: they all stole a little winter coal. "This was how we got our winter coal," said about everyone. Great Grandmother Adelaide needed coal as well as Grandmother, so everyone worked picking up coal.

In my very early life, the horses, Old Frank and Old Jack, just never seemed to share my joy of seeing the wagon in use. I liked everything from watching the horses being harnessed to the first rolling step. I would set on the seat any time the old thing moved, and I would stay right there until I was told to go on off and start loading. Now, I was truly the rightful Little King Fat Boy on the hill. Except, a horse fart is just about the worse kind of fart there is. You have got to be careful, because if you get that smell on you or in your hair it is going to take lye soap to get it out!

Back in my earlier life I had an old school bus parked along the river. Through the years the "old bus" has become a landmark for those of us living along the River Ridge. From the old bus, the road was a right easy, but steady uphill, pull. I could even ride the wagon up about the pond. There I got off and joined the men walking alongside of the wagon. It was a steady walk up and across the railroad and up through May's Holler on around the pond on the old car road to the barn. It was not hard on Fred and Jack to make two or even three trips a day. One of the brothers and me would bring the ear corn to the barn and pile it up in the corner, while the two other brothers stayed at the river bottom to shuck corn from dry fodder shocks. Sometimes five or six fodder shocks would be tied onto the wagon and hauled to the barn or Uncle Nelson's. The milk cows just seemed to love corn stalks. I was never permitted to ride the wagon back to the barn. "Too hard on them horses to pull us too." the men would say.

But the pull up from the Tommy Bottom was a man-and-boy-killing walk. Every inch of that hill was steep. Even I knew that the horses were in for a hard afternoon and would earn their keep. Sometimes they worked up a sweating lather coming up the hill. My job was to carry small blocks of wood; Daddy did, too. When Uncle Nelson or Shorty stopped the wagon to give the horses a rest, we placed the blocks behind the wheels to keep the wagon from rolling off backwards down the hill. Everything was hard work, but it was also more fun than about anything. Once we got to the top and Fred and Jack cooled off some, we would all pile on the wagon for the slow rhythmic walk down the road to home. The metal horseshoes made a click-clacking sound. Boys and girls watched us pass. I just knew they were saying to themselves, "Damn, that looks like fun, and who is the short, kind of fat little man setting there smiling like a boar coon?" Yes, that would be me!

Everyone on the hill used the old wagon, and the old horses, too. I'm not sure, but I think the wagon was sold to Luther Snider when I was little boy. I do know that Daddy traded Old Fred to Mr. Luther for a piece of ground to build our home on. Mr. Luther used the wagon to pull small haystacks to the barn, most of the time by putting a rope over the hay. I liked riding on the haystacks a lot, too, but not like riding the old wagon. From the first time I saw the wagon until the last time I saw it could not have been more than two or three years. After that people had trucks, and horse-drawn things were just set up to rot and rust away.

When I was teenager, the only thing left in Mr. Luther's barn were the wooden wheels. We just stacked hay over them. At the time, I never gave it one thought. Kevin says he still has a metal rim from the wagon wheels. I am sure he will keep it and not let The Woolf have it. Woolf would make a saw, a bunch of knives or even a gun out of it. And the memory would just be gone forever.

In truth, I cannot remember exactly who owned the old wagon. It may have belonged to Shorty and Nelson. Mr. Luther may have been the owner all along. It doesn't really matter. I just loved setting behind those big horses.

Walking the Cow to Morey Long's

Never start the dogs down the branch, always start um up the branch. A coon is a sight lighter when you are carrying him downhill.

Daddy, Uncle Shorty and Uncle Nelson all had milk cows. Each year they were turned off dry in late fall, and there would be a lesser amount of fresh milk and cottage cheese until Flower had her calf and came to her milk. You did not want both cows to go dry at the same time. If you did this there would be no milk for a month or two.

In June or July of each year Flower had to be walked over to Mr. Morey Long's to be serviced by his bull. They never were "bred"; the milk cow got "serviced"! In mixed company, you just never spoke of the cow being bred. No one ever said that Flower is in heat and ready to be bred. I think that girls and women are not supposed to know about such things. This here was real man stuff. She always was serviced, unless children were present. Then, Bessie or Flower (they were the milk cows) "went over to visit" Mr. Long's bull. You know, like they were going to play a few hands of rummy or compare each other's pasture or something. Maybe they were going talk about the weather the way men on the River Ridge did. After my uncles had had a few cold Blue Ribbons I got to learn a whole different language—the language only full-grown men know and are privileged to speak. Birds and bees were not part of this conversation at all, but them rascals were certainly present during these discussions.

Well, I did not mind walking the cow over to Mr. Long's. I just never looked forward to it much. I do not think that a halter-broken cow would have been welcome on River Ridge. To get the cow to Mr. Long's farm I somehow had to get a halter on the cow. Oh, she was already in the mood to make the trip. The halter was to slow her down some and to help me try to keep up with her some. Some is the operative word here. On the way over, I partly ran and was partly dragged. Partly, I just chased after old Flower. Both me and the cow ran the whole way as fast as we could go. She would not stop for nothing. I had to make sure she was pointed at the gate through the fence. If I did not do this, there was going to be hole in the fence to fix. An old cow with courting on her mind is the most ornery and most unpredictable thing there is.

Once we got to Mr. Long's, I was to set around and watch the cow get bred and pay Mr. Long two dollars and then start the trip back. Sometimes we just left the milk cow for a few days. Going over was a kind of fast and rough trip. Coming back to the barn was the exact opposite. It was slow and would make every muscle in my body ache. Once I got the halter on Flower, she would lock up her legs and not move. The harder I pulled, the longer her neck got, but her feet were still right where we started. After a lot of pulling and getting behind her and pushing, she would take a step or two. From Mr. Long's back up over the hill wasn't more than a mile. But pulling, pushing and carrying a milk cow, it is long way up through the woods. Here is the real killer. By the time we passed the gate in Mr. Snider's field and the barn was in sight, Flower just seemed to be halter broken. She would walk beside me. Every once in a while, she would stop and crop of a mouth full of clover. A twitch on the rope, and she walked closer to home.

I was asked why we turned the cow off to go dry. Flower was in the later stage of pregnancy. This means the baby calf she was carrying was growing. More energy was need for the calf's development. As Daddy and Shorty said, "Flower just needs a break from making milk, so the calf will be healthy and strong." After the calf was born there was plenty milk.

The very minute the calf was born, all the kids and adults went to look at it and to pet it. If the calf was a bull, we were never allowed to play too much. Daddy said, "It may make Flower go dry if you play with a calf too much." He did not want me to get too attached to a calf that was going to market very quickly.

Some bull calves were put in real little wooden pens, so small that they could not even turn around in. These were veal calves. Some were sold, and others made their way to our supper table. If the calf was a heifer, we could play some, because there was a chance we were just might keep her or sell her locally to someone for a milk cow. A good, well-broke calf sells a little better than a harder-headed one. We would make hay string halters for her and lead her around like a dog. When she got sold or carried off, it would almost make you cry.

The Old Cream-Colored Bus

I WANTED TO WRITE THIS STORY because the memory of the old White Arrow Bus is just about gone. Truly, the old bus and public transportation from McCoy to Blacksburg and VPI were so far ahead of their time that it isn't funny. When most people think of public transportation, they think of city buses, subways and trains. Not me. I think of an old cream-colored bus. Monday through Friday it ran past my house. I liked to look out the window and see it. When it passed, I would just wonder where those people were going off to. Today, wouldn't it be great if you could get on a bus in McCoy or Wake Forest or Long Shop or Prices Fork and ride all the way to Blacksburg or to Virginia Tech? That would be a boon for college students and old people up and down the river.

Telling this story just may be like putting together a jigsaw puzzle with a few pieces missing. I just might have to take a little writer's license to fill in the gaps, but I am going to try to be as close to the true story of the *White Arrow* as possible.

Sadly, most of the people who rode this bus are now very old or have gone on to much bigger bus rides in the sky. Some just can't remember it. Not long ago, I asked one of my siblings about her memories of the

79

old *White Arrow Bus System*. She told me that she had no memories of the old bus at all. I think this is true of most people.

Until I started writing this, I had not given the old bus any thought for years. Those last memories occurred more than 1,000 miles from my beloved River Ridge and more than 40 years ago. It all happened when I attended the University of Rhode Island. The university was in the town of Kingston, and I lived in the small community of Narragansett close to the Atlantic Ocean. Most days, I drove to school, but on this particular day I rode the bus.

I am standing on a Rhode Island Public Transportation bus headed inland to the University. I am not a half-mile from the Atlantic Ocean. Holy Macaroni! I am riding up the hurricane escape road on the *Narragansett*. The road is as straight as a Baptist preacher and wider than Old Miss Cadle's butt. It was constructed after a major hurricane in the 1920s, when many people lost their lives because there were no large roads leading inland. As the *Narragansett* hums and sways along, my mind starts to wander and ends up on the "Old Cream Bus."

Since the *White Arrow* was a bus I never actually got to ride, I am only guessing here, but I think this story started in the spring of 1956 and that would make me only 5 years old! You know it takes something right strong to make a 5-year-old remember, unless it's food. That is why I needed to ask some people who would have been 7 or 8 years old at the time the old bus was running. They can remember a lot more, but few had any memory at all. I also asked my mother, Ruth Lytton. She rode the bus to town for groceries, and once in a while to visit the doctor or to take care of family business. Earlier on, both Aunt Edith and Tib rode the bus to work at VPI.

Jane McCoy just might have the best memory. Her daddy drove the old bus, and she used the *White Arrow* as her playhouse when her daddy wasn't driving it. In summers, Jane even made the trips with her daddy. She said that she loved riding along. One of her last memories of the *White Arrow* came while she was watching "The Waltons" on television. She realized that when John Boy went off to college he rode on a *White Arrow Lines* bus just like her daddy's.

The *White Arrow* picked up people in McCoy then turned down into Wake Forest. Back in the 1950s, true to the times all over the South, black folks from Wake Forest had to sit in the back of the bus. As soon as Miss Cornelia Adams got on the bus, Jane got up from her seat up front and went to the back of the bus to sit on Miss Cornelia's lap. Miss Cornelia held her all the way to her (Miss Cornelia's) stop. Then Jane went back up front and sat behind her father's seat.

I named the *White Arrow* "The Old Cream Bus." Please keep in mind that I was little and could not read the name on the side. Since it was painted kind of a cream color on the top and lighter green on the bottom, I guess that was the first thing that came into my smallish mind. It wasn't until years later when the bus sat in Buford McCoy's junkyard that I saw it was the *White Arrow*.

I can remember standing with Momma and Grandmother out at the road by the mailbox waiting for the bus to town. When the bus stopped, Momma would get on and leave me standing. When I bleated "I want to go to town, too," Grandmother would hold me by the shirt collar and say, "You are just too little to ride your Old Cream Bus, so you just hush now."

I feel it is important to re-inform you that I never rode on the cream bus. Mother said, "You are just too little and squirm too much; having you on the bus would be too much of an aggravation." She also admitted it was nice to just get off River Ridge and go to town by herself for a little while. Now at four or five years of age, I could not have been that much trouble, could I?

To my recollection, the bus was about a late 1930s or real early 1940s Dodge. It did not look so much like an old retired school bus as like an old used-up city bus. Everyone agreed that if you wanted a ride, all you had to do was stand by the mailbox and get your ticket punched. I guess you could pay cash money, too.

Alba "Bush" Albert drove from McCoy to Blacksburg everyday Monday through Friday. In 1948, my family rode the *White Arrow* to Blacksburg for 15 cents morning and evening to work at VPI. She said there were no official bus stops. You just stood by the road and Bush stopped; he kind of knew everyone. She echoed what my mother said: "In 1952, the bus was almost never full. Everyone was starting to get cars, and the old bus's days were numbered."

Some people living in Blacksburg and up and down the River Ridge Road took the *White Arrow* to work. Some might have even have ridden the bus to work in the McCoy Coal Mines, while others rode from Blacksburg to visit family. I spoke with Marie Bland and her son, my most particular friend, Jimmy. Mrs. Bland grew up in McCoy, but lived all of her adult life in Blacksburg. She said she often rode the bus home to McCoy. In or about 1956, Mrs. Bland would put Jimmy, at the ripe old age of six, on the bus to go visit his grandmother in McCoy. Jimmy said he could remember those trips just like they were yesterday. "Nothing against that bus, but I just hated those trips. Almost with certainty, I was going to be carsick either coming or going, sometimes both ways."

After World War II, some people had cars but not everyone. People now wanted to go out and were not as content to stay put as they had been before and during the war. So the bus truly did help a lot. As for me, I can only remember standing by the mailbox with Mamaw holding me by my shirt collar.

In interviewing people who are known to have ridden the old *White Arrow*, I have learned three different scenarios as to three different routes it took. I now think that all three just might be true at different times. Below is the one I heard most often.

During the regular workday, Mr. Bush Albert was employed by the College (Virginia Polytechnic Institute or VPI). We locals just shortened it down to The College. Again, Mr. Albert was employed full-time by The College and was the part-time driver of the White Arrow. Before work each morning, he made his run picking up people and then made one pass through downtown Blacksburg. After work in the afternoon, he retraced his path picking up people and returning them to their mailboxes. Some said he also drove to Christiansburg, and others thought he even went all the way to Parrott. So, the Old Cream Bus was the way that a lot of people got around. By the time I was getting big enough to know things and understand some, I could see the bus's days were numbered. It seemed like every day or two there was a new car blowing its horn at me. Then one day it was no longer profitable for Mr. Alba "Bush" Albert, and he went out of business. Mom said that lots of people up and down the road were just at a loss for transportation. Now everybody needed cars. Now, for the first time, Momma just felt stuck on River Ridge.

In the fall of 1971, I was working on the farm down at Whitethorn. The whole farm was caught up in chopping corn silage. All of a sudden, the old 1946 Chevrolet dump truck broke down. We called all over the countryside looking for replacement parts. No one had any suggestions of where to even look. The old truck was just a worn out old antique itself.

We went to see Mr. Buford and started crying the blues to him. "We have just got to get the corn chopped. It is getting dryer by the day, and we do not have a truck to haul corn silage on."

He stroked his chin. "Well, I do not have a truck and do not know where you could borrow one, but if you are up to it, the parts you are looking for are somewhere down there in the *Arrow.*"

You could see the top of the old bus from the road, but getting there was totally a different story. We waded through green briers, young locust trees and thousands upon thousands of unseen and unheard snakes of every kind. But we got there. The old *White*

Arrow had been used as a storage unit in the junkyard. We took to carrying out car rear ends, everything from very old truck parts to engine blocks and other old antique things. I do not have a clue what they were. Every kind of old spring shackle ever made was in the old bus. There was about one of everything.

True to Buford's word, about halfway back in the bus laid a used part for a 1946 Chevrolet dump truck. Somehow we dragged it out and put all of the automotive museum parts back into the bus for safe keeping. Thanks to the pack rat tendency of an old mechanic, the generosity of one Buford McCoy and the durability of the Old Cream Bus, within a day we were back chopping silage. The Old Cream Bus just kind of knew that someday I would come. The bus and me, well we both hoped it would be for a ride, but even then I just took for granted the significance of the day.

For many years. I drove past the Old Cream Bus sitting and rotting away in the weeds by Buford's Garage. After a while, the words *White Arrow Lines* were replaced by rust. I very often thought, "What a waste." Some old school buses found their way to the banks of New River. There they became a home away from home for Huckleberry Finn wannabes. Some of the old buses were purchased by local men and got themselves converted into real fancy campers. Those received new big eight-cylinder engines, magnificent multiple layered paint jobs of colorful, faraway scenes painted on their sides, and clean, carpeted interiors. They truly were Winnebagos long before Winnebagos were even thought of. But the Old Cream Bus, why it spent its last days and years alone, slowly rusting away and then vanishing in Buford's weeds. One day, as I drove by, I noticed it was just gone. Possibly, the car crusher had come along and hauled it away for scrap iron.

Me, I just watched it go up and down the road morning and evening. I also watched it stop coming. Then it was gone, and as quickly as I learned it was there, it just faded away forever. It could have added some color to this little piece of River Ridge history and my understanding of public transportation. But then I was only five years old.

Eat, Drink and Be Wary

Shorty and Onions

AN ALTERNATE TITLE for this little ditty could be "Onions and Their Many Uses." You see, Uncle Shorty planted lots of onions. In the spring, he had a smell of onions about him. Not an offensive smell, but a light smell, unmistakably of onions. He never planted less than eight, sometimes as many as ten rows of onions in the garden. He took care to place the little onion sets no less than one inch apart. I think he wanted to make sure there were plenty.

The big garden right behind the house is where the onions and cabbage were planted. You wanted them right close to your dining table. We ate green onions and salt at every meal. Before you went to bed, you sliced up small, tender green onions and put them on top of your dish of buttermilk and corn-bread. They were so good, all covered in black pepper, it makes me salivate just to write this down,.

For breakfast, we cooked onions with eggs or ate them raw. Onion and butter biscuits were also a mainstay for lunch. For supper, the rules say that you can eat them about any way you like. For example, you could warm them up in homemade sauerkraut with cornbread. They were real tasty that way. You could eat them with scalded lettuce—hard to beat that way. I even had onions lightly softened, tops and all, in sausage grease once or twice. Now that was eating like the rich people did in the city. The more I think about, it everyone walked around with a light smell of onion on them. Me included!

Well, back to the point of this little story. I rode Old Bus 8, the "Hammer Head" Lucas school bus from McCoy. I got off at the Prices Fork Elementary School. "Hammer Head" went on to Blacksburg High School with all the big kids from McCoy and Long Shop. The Town of Blacksburg was somewhere far away in my knowing of stuff then. I asked Mrs. Gwynn one day about high school and she said, "Some learn about high school, and some just learn about the back woods. Fourth grade is still being discussed for you; so don't get your hopes up for high school or the fourth grade, for that matter. You ain't got the third grade whipped yet." Yessir, poor Old Mrs. Gwynn, she was a true charmer and an eloquent orator she was. So the trip from River Ridge to Prices Fork would be enough to keep my attention, and I would just let the fourth grade come if that was in the bigger plan.

The bus was so crowded that you could hardly find a place to stand. By the time it stopped at my house, you had no chance of finding a place to sit. When we got past Lovers' Leap we were packed in like sardines. On Thanksgiving and near to Christmas, a lot of the 16- and 17-year-old boys and girls who had dropped out of school came back for the day. When everyone got mashed on you and everything kind of got heated up a little, body odor came oozing out. Not one of us had any *Old Spice* on or would have known what it was or how to use it. Regularly, there were times when I held my breath for 25 or 30 minutes as the bus moved up the River Ridge Road. My grade school teacher, Old Miss Maude McLeary, told us not to hold our breath for long periods of time, because it just might affect our brains. So every once in while I just had to take a short breath; but I did not want to chance a breath too often. Easy for her to say; she never rode Bus 8 with them older kids.

I was right big for my age, and on most days I was about one head above the direct contact with the stench. But it was still mighty strong up where I was. One particular morning I was all squeezed up with a nice, pretty, little fourth-grade girl from Prices Fork. She was about chest high to me and in direct contact with the big kids. She looked up at me with them real big sad brown eyes and said: "You have got to change places with me, please. I am stuck right in someone's stinking arm pit." I knew that from that very day forward I was destined to become a true Southern Gentleman. My next movement might have been as worthy a gesture as Atticus shooting the hydrophobic dog in *To Kill A Mockingbird*. We took to squirming until we had changed places. Oh my goodness, no one can know just how much difference one inch or two can make. Holy Macaroni, possibly all of the wiggling and squirming had shaken out some brand new kind of body odors.

I needed advice on how to deal with the teenaged body odor on the bus, so I took this issue to the highest order of thinking that I knew—Uncle Shorty. To my way of thinking he knew everything. In fact, he did know these families, and he said about all of them had a problem with fear of soap and water. I suggested that I not take a bath for a few weeks and just pay them back. At that point, Mod Snider also started offering suggestions. He said, "Going dirty for a few weeks is not the answer; oh Lordy oh Lordy no!

Cawliga, you keep taking baths for our sake."

But Shorty did give me one good suggestion: "When you see the bus come around the curve at Sam Smith's, eat yourself eight or ten good-sized green onions fresh right out of the garden. Then them other kids will let you stand anywhere you want. You eat the onion tops as well, and 'Hammer Head' will even let you drive the damn bus home."

I never did this. I got to thinking that the treatment might be as bad as the cure. You see, them older boys and girls were already into onion-eating. Their breath was about as strong as their body odor. They seemed to get you coming and going. Another thing was, every time one of the big boys or girls acted up "Hammer Head" always hollered at one of the little kids. I think he was scared of them big kids, just like I was. So, if I had eaten the onions, he may have made me stand by them all the way to school.

He could not make me stand by them on the way home, because after lunch the big kids just slipped out the back door of the schoolhouse or climbed through a window and went home. No one ever went to look for them either! I mean no one, *ever.* You could tell when they were gone, because the classroom teacher opened the windows and the door to the hall. Even at Christmas time when it was cold, the place got a real good airing out. She never said anything. Medium-sized kids said the teacher was catching them hot flashes. I know better. She was not flashing anything or we would have seen it; she had had a full dose of teenaged body odor and onion breath and was too scared to tell the dirty rascals to go home and take a bath. Pretty much the whole schoolhouse got a good airing out.

Friends, Just Be Watchful

ALL I AM SAYING IS just keep your eyes on your friends. You just never know what is going through their evil minds. No sir, you just never know. It is the summer of 1968. Chuck, Jimmy and me are picking up hay on the Obenchain Farm, just outside of Blacksburg. It is just a little hotter than three kinds of hell, and the water in the gallon jug is warm and in limited supply. It is so hot that I have left my best pipe on the dashboard of Chuck's old Ford truck. It is just too heavy to carry.

After a while, all of the wagons and trucks are loaded, and it is time to start for the barn. I climb in the cab of the truck with Chuck and Jimmy. They are both real quiet, a little too quiet. It is just too hot to talk, so I pick up my old pipe, hold a match over the bowl and draw down deep. Damn this tobacco is strong and right down nasty. It won't stay lit, either. I cough a few times, then put a match over the bowl a second time. I suck on the stem real hard. I say, "Damn! Leaving this pipe out in the hot sun has made the tobacco go bad."

About this time both Chuck and Jimmy start to laugh. Not just a chuckle either; it is a deep-down, gut-wrenching laugh that just would not stop.

I sit there looking at them. I have no clue what the joke is, so I go back to trying to get my pipe to light. The laughter just gets worse. After a few minutes everything settles down, and they tell me they have knocked the tobacco out of my pipe and filled it with dried-up Japanese beetles from the truck's dash.

Yep, keep your eyes on your friends. You just never know what is going through their evil minds. The worst part of this is every summer since smoking them Japanese beetles, I have had a strong urge to eat the leaves off of grape vines.

The Pear Tree in the Hollow

Always look for the good, it is there.

I JUST LOVE TO EAT PEARS. Even today when I go to the store, I always load up on pears first and apples second. When I was a child, we always had lots of pears. There was one real big tree down in the holler. These pears were harder than Chinese arithmetic, and that is hardest kind of arithmetic there is. If you tried to eat them when they were green, you just might lose a tooth. The old tree stood just below the pond and up from the potato patch. In the fall, I would race the rabbits for bites of good unbruised pears. When I got a little older I would take Old Fanny—she was an older gentle horse—and the sled to the holler and bring back a horse sled full of pears.

I would pick up all the solid pears and bruised pears from the ground and climb up the tree and pick what I could. Sometimes Daddy or Shorty or Nelson would stand below me to catch them so they would not get bruised up. "Pick all the green pears you can. They will last longer." The badly bruised ones went to the hogs. The unbruised ones were wrapped in newspaper and put in the cellar for winter. The others were pealed and cooked on the wood cook stove in two or three large pots to make pear butter. It was like making apple butter; just on a smaller scale.

95

Some were baked. Some were stewed down until they were in thick pear juice. A few of the better ones were canned. In these days, if an empty jar was around, something was found to fill it.

I know that it doesn't sound like much, but to me it was a great thing. I got to harness the horse by myself. I went off and did what I thought of as real man's work. Me and Grandmother set on stools on the porch and peeled pears. It was a good time. When the Christmas snow was on the hills, digging through the newspapers for a ripe, mellow, yellow pear was great. Better than eating a candy bar. I could set in the cool musty cellar and eat a pear, and the juices would run off my fat little chin. Few times have I ever been truly happier. I just don't do things like that anymore and why I do not know!

One of the funniest things I ever saw was my brother trying to imitate the pony that had eaten a whole pear and did not chew it up first. The pony coughed, wheezed and stumbled around trying to either get that pear to go on down his throat or to spit it out of his mouth. My brother thought the pony was truly going to die. After a while the pony just stopped coughing and gagging and went right back to grazing them hard old pears. Me, I ate them too and just loved the feel of them in my hands and the smell in the cellar. Yes, I stood by the pony and waited for a pear to fall.

Chinquapins and a Bad Trick

*Once you go and squeeze out the toothpaste,
you just cannot put it back in the tube.*

WHEN I WAS A KID, every once in while I would hear one of the grownups talk about someone playing a prank. They had an expression that told the listener just how severe the prank was. "Why, that sorry rascal must have stayed up most of the night to have dreamed up that trick." This particular trick came to me on a Sunday afternoon when I was picking chinquapins. Jimmy Bland and I were over in Craig County up on State Route 42. We needed a full gallon or so of chinquapins so we could watch the Sunday afternoon football game.

There was this rather talkative fellow in my high school study hall. He just talked all the time, and this kept me from sleeping. Back then I did not worry about studying; I just concentrated on sleeping. I am going to call this talkative person Robert. Yes, Robert will do just fine; come to think of it, he looked like a Robert! Well, Robert started talking as soon as I set down.

"What are you eating?"

"These are chinquapins. Picked out the burs myself."

I gave old Robert a few, and he did enjoy eating them. I know this because he told me so right in the middle of some of his talking!

I gave him a few more and then told him that I had run out. But I did have a few almonds in my pocket. I discovered Robert loved almonds, too. He liked them a lot. I know because he told me so, a lot! I munched down on a few more, and Robert stuck his hand over the back of my seat wanting some more. So, I reached in my shirt pocket and handed him a few more. But, what I gave him wasn't almonds. They were freshly cracked out peach pits. Old Robert chomped down on the peach pits, and he went to screaming for water. He took off running, and I settled back to eating my chinquapins and laughing uncontrollably.

In just a few minutes order was restored. Robert's tongue had relaxed some. I had stopped my uncontrollable laughter. No one else in the auditorium had a clue what happened. I knew his tongue was ok, because he started to cuss. I did not know that town boys could cuss like that. The more I laughed, the more he cussed. I think that he went on to look for his own chinquapins. If he did, I would have been scared to eat them.

Today, when someone pulls a trick on me, I try to laugh right along with them. Well some of the time anyway.

The Biggie Bird

ACCORDING TO GRANDMOTHER, there was a time when the family rented space to a bunch of immigrants to build a tent camp. This camp was located down in May's Holler just below the present-day pond. Today, there are only a few ditches or wagon ruts marking the site. These people were the laborers working to build the Virginian Railroad. They were said to be from Poland. From what I was told, not many of them spoke any good American, and they were always hungry. Few had small gardens, and they always needed meat to eat. One day, a couple of the women were at Great Grandmother's house telling her a story about one of the men shooting a big turkey. The women took the bird, cleaned it and cooked it. As they described it, "The biggie bird tasted like shit." They had shot a turkey buzzard thinking it was a turkey. They went back to eating rabbits, birds and groundhogs. Mr. Sam Smith once said that they ate every robin they could catch. But no one ate any more turkey buzzards.

By the 1930s the railroad had been built, and the Polish people had moved on. From the late 50s to the early 60s, I can remember one immigrant family still came to visit. They parked their camper under the big white oak behind our house and stayed for a week or so before they moved on. Mamaw said, "They like the place, because the Lyttons were good to them. This was their first American home, and they have pleasant memories of being treated good." Shorty and Daddy called them a bunch of roaming gypsies. Uncle Nelson said some of them found their way to Detroit and went to work in the car plants up there. Seems this struck a tender nerve with some on River Ridge, because the Poles might have moved up in the world, so to speak. One had an Airstream camper. They just ran off and left my family setting on the hill.

By the time the Poles left, new things had come along to watch along the old road. Uncle Lake told me that every summer a prison work gang was unloaded first at Whitethorn, and then after a few days, at our mailbox. They walked over the hill to continue their job, which was to cut the railroad right-of-way, all the way to Pepper. Each man wore ankle shackles with a 30-foot piece of chain attached and hooked to the man behind him.

Uncle Lake said they would spread out all in unison with scythe in hand. Each made a cut, stepped forward, then bent over and moved his chain. This would go on for hours. Slowly, but surely, every weed, stick or small tree was cut. If one man needed to pee, everyone got to pee. If one needed to do other things, he was unlocked from the chain to do his business. But every man had to cut extra to make up for the missing man. Lake said yellow jackets and hornets gave the prisoners fits, and it was comical to see chained men swat bees with mowing scythes while trying to run all chained together. Back then, the right-of-way was kept clean from rail to fence. It made a great summer pasture for the Lyttons' cows and horses.

Red Coon Is a Real Good Chew

In my day I have chewed a lot of tobacco, and I have enjoyed about all of it. I think that I would still chew tobacco today if it did not make me sick. About every kind of chewing tobacco has memories associated with it. For example, I guess I have chewed possibly a half-million plugs, but no more than that, of *Day's Work*. When I was in the seventh or eighth grade in school, I had been home sick a few days before Elmer, my father, brought me a twelve cut box of *Day's Work*. I think this was to cheer me up and make me feel better. Mama Ruth said, "You have been sick with stuff running out of both ends of you. You start chewing that stuff, and it's hard to tell what is going to happen to you." I do remember having a real weak stomach.

Not following my mother's sound advice, I peeled off the paper and that brown wrapping. I took myself a good solid chew. I carefully started to working it up. I got the cud to the point that I needed to spit; so I rallied myself from my chair and went outside. I did this a few times. The more I chewed, the more I enjoyed the plug. After awhile, I took a brand new chew and started over on working the cud up. After about an hour I started to feel bad, and after about another hour I was just plain sick. I thought I was going to vomit up my toenails. Mom was compassionate about this: "You big dummy, I told you this would happen." Then she just walked away and left me in misery.

From that day forward, I just could not chew *Day's Work*. It made me think of the taste of linseed oil. Still, I kept on chewing other kinds of tobacco up until my teeth were just about worn off. But no more *Day's Work*. Even to this day the smell of the stuff just does me in. My yarning about this is just trying to set the stage for what comes next.

Even today, once in a while, I will buy a plug of *Red Coon*. It is one of the best things you can do when you're squirrel hunting. There is just something about that tobacco and bitter licorice taste I always enjoyed.

I think I was either an eighth grader or a freshman in high school. Probably it was the eighth grade, because by the ninth grade I was starting to get a lot smarter about being around them town folks. Anyway, in English class every afternoon right after lunch, about all of us boys who had graduated from Prices Forks Elementary School settled back for a relaxing chew. We were all in English class together, so this was where we chewed.

As a general rule, each boy had a pop bottle that he spit in. One day "Bird Shot" did not have a pop bottle, so he just spit in his desk. I told him after class that I thought that was a bad idea, because the janitor would someday have to clean that desk. In the past, at Prices Fork Elementary, we had just spit out the window when we did not have a pop bottle. No one ever said a word, provided the window was open.

There was one time a boy named Gary Martin forgot to look at the window and spit on it, so he had to clean it up. No one spit out the window or chewed for a few weeks. But we were more cultured now. We would look at the window first. We had learned that town and high school chewing had a new set of rules.

The next day Miss Ruby White, the English teacher, started a new teaching method. She always reminded me of a green bean: tall and very thin and bent some near to the top of her. Well, she took to randomly calling on people, just asking them to answer a question out loud or even read the questions to the class. Again, Bird Shot did not have a pop bottle, but his jaw looked like he was holding a golf ball. Miss White asked, "Well, Mr. Bird Shot, would you please read the paragraph to the class and give us your interpretation?"

He looked from one person to the next. With all the eyes right on him, he could not spit into the desk. Why he did not just stand up and spit out the open window is beyond me. Instead, Bird Shot straightened up his neck and swallowed the cud of tobacco.

It looked like a large bolus slowly working itself down his neck. He coughed a few times, tried to speak a few times, gasped for air a few times, gagged a few times, then ran from the class as fast he could go. The whole class turned to watch Bird Shot go down the hall. The rest of us spit hard a few times. We were ready for the barrage of questions and reading. A boy named Bill was sent to check on Bird Shot. His story of what went on in the bathroom was not pretty. When they came out, they were both pale as ghosts. We did not partake of any more *Red Coon* during English class. But the laughter went on for weeks.

The only thing that broke the tobacco laughter was me picking up a book from the floor. As I have stated earlier, I was large for my age. I could outgrow a pair of blue jeans in just a few weeks, but I just kept on wearing them even if they were small and too tight. Another thing—how do I say this? I still had not mastered the manly art of wearing underwear. They just seemed to ride up on me and make me feel bunched up or something. One afternoon, one of the students dropped her book in front of me, and I bent over to pick it up. My jeans split from the zipper all the way back around to my belt. This was real embarrassing. But not as embarrassing as having to hear someone say, "Why, that rascal doesn't have on any drawers." Now the whole class broke into a loud laughing uproar.

I did not have a clue what to do. Walter Price, the assistant principal, came to my rescue. I took my shirt off and wrapped it around my naked butt and walked to his office. Mr. Price gave me the keys to his personal car, a great big Dodge station wagon, and told me to go home a get a new pair of pants. Plus, he told me to put on some underwear.

They don't make teachers like that anymore. First off, he out-laughed the student body. Once he had regained his composure, he started moving students on to their respective classrooms, except for those that wanted to stay laugh some more. Notice, that rather than start lecturing me, he handed me the keys to his personal car and told to go home and change clothes.

Well, to say the least, Buck Shot was off the hook. His *Red Coon* debacle was over. My baring of my butt was the main thing laughed about for a few weeks. There are people who make an impact on your life, and you don't know it at the time. Mr. Walter was just a wonderful teacher and a fine man!

Mrs. Helen Walkers saw the whole thing and enjoyed a few laughs too. She was always trying to get the best of me. She did this day. She was funny, too; she never forgave me for being smart. I never did one piece of homework for her English class. I just refused to do any class assignments. I did take the test, and I pretty much always made an A. The class was studying Shakespeare. On the final exam for the year, the question was, "How did Birnam Wood come to the Dunsinane Castle?" I wrote a full page on this. I spoke of witches' predictions and using camouflage to sneak up on the castle. Mrs. Walkers did not know that I had read Shakespeare. "Why, only town boys seem to know these things," she said.

I just went back to sleep. I got my D and moved on. She did not know that I read books setting on the river bank at the bus. Long before school started in the fall, I had read and fished away lots of books, including my high school literature book.

The Old Duck Hunt as I Was Told

PAPPY TOLD THIS TALE over and over. My uncles did too, so I think there is a lot of truth in it. Somewhere around 1930 I think, Daddy would help someone that lived along the lower end of the Whitethorn Community with their duck hunting. For the life of me, I cannot put a name on the man in this story. I only know that he lived near Cowan Siding. He either worked on the farm at Whitethorn or lived in one of the old company houses near Mr. Whit's or around the old hotel near the train station. But, I am working on remembering it. Well anyway, Pappy said that this event took place on the Cowan Farm at Whitethorn. This is the present-day Virginia Tech Research Farm.

Daddy would gather up corn stalks in early fall and build a sturdy duck blind around a heavy bench. The blind was built to look like a real big corn shock with a room inside. Person X had a small cannon gun, as Daddy called it, mounted on the bench. In later stories told by Shorty, Lake, Nelson, and others, the gun took on the name "Blunder Bust." All of my uncles told about the same story in one way or another, so there must be more than a grain of truth in it.

I have since seen examples of a gun like this on the Discovery Channel on television. It looked much like the one used by Elmer Fudd in cartoons. Today these large guns are outlawed, but there are still many examples in museums.

When the ducks started to come in and feed in the cornfields, you would put out very small amounts of corn as bait, scattering it in a spot the exact size of the spread of the shot. The objective was to kill as many as you could in one shot. You fed the ducks a little every day, just about daylight. And every morning they would come to the blind first to feed. One morning before daylight, Person X loaded the big shot gun with old nails, bolts, small round rocks, pieces of old wire fencing and any other thing he could find. When the duck numbers were at their maximum around the blind, he fired the "Blunder Bust," maybe killing 30 or 40 at one time. The next morning he started baiting the ducks again.

Back during the Great Depression, people ate what they could find and made money where they could. For a while, they shipped salted ducks in wooden barrels all picked and cleaned for city people too lazy to hunt their own. Today, I lean a little more toward fresh killed.

Making Molasses and You Go, Girl!

*Time is going to change on you and you will have to
stop and think back just to remember what was work
and what was fun. You just wait and see if'n you
don't often find them to be the same thing. Well, that
was what Mr. Luther thought.*

NEVER DOES A SATURDAY MORNING in the fall pass
that I do not think about this story. The sausage is
all fried, the eggs are just about ready to come off the
stove, and pancakes are stacked up seven or eight
high. All of a sudden, I go looking for the syrup and
butter, and I have to just stop the search and chuckle
to myself.

Well Elmer, he was my father, always wanted
us kids to see and do lots of things that he had done
and experienced growing up. "One of these days, and
not too far off, no one around will even know what I
am talking about. These little things will be just in
the past and gone forever." So to this end, we raised
bottle lambs plus calves on a bottle, and planted and
worked big gardens. We raised rabbits, chickens and
even pheasants. "If'n it can grow, we grew it. If you can
shoot it, we shot it. Then we ate it too. Someday you
will be glad you did these things," Daddy would say.

Into the "Going to Experience Things" category
I must place making molasses. Now, I admit I eat a

little less than a cup or two of molasses a year. I put a spoonful in my baked beans. I will ever so lightly drizzle a few of them molasses across a stack of well-buttered pancakes. If I forget to eat them this year, it is ok with me. It ain't no great loss.

When this all started I was about 20 years old and had spent almost my whole life working on all the local farms. But, at this point I had done moved on to town work. I was now employed by the Mick-or-Mack Grocery Store. This was inside work, where there was no sunburn or sweat running down the crack of my butt and no working nine or ten days a week in just seven days. I was now a town working man! (I would have just loved to work down at the Piggly Wiggly, but we did not have one anymore. It had closed a few years earlier.) Well, I was old enough to know that there wasn't going to be any fun coming out of this molasses venture at all. All I could see was some hard-assed work and a lot of sweat. Oh hell, here we go!

In early spring we drove a short distance over to a Mr. Placer Worlds' house. He lived so far back in the country that he would have had to drive to town to go fishing. I knew exactly where we were going. Our old school bus bounced over the deep holes in the road every day to pick up his granddaughter. For a fat little boy like me it was worth the ride. Tammy Worlds was right pretty and a real quiet girl, too.

Old Mr. Worlds was no less than 85 or 90 years old. I do not think that he was already 100, but every one of them deep wrinkles in his face showed that he was very old. Still, he had a quick wit, and his eyes were bright and set real close over his big nose. After a long while of setting around in the kitchen talking, a few stiff drinks were taken, and a deal was struck to use the old man's cane mill and molasses pan. We walked out into an overgrown field, and Mr. Worlds stuck out his bony finger toward a clump of locust trees and blackberry briers. "The mill is in the clump of brush," he said.

"What in the hell have you done got us into?" I screeched.

Elmer answered, "Just you take time, boy, this will all work out. You just wait and see."

Truly, we set to work on the brush pile with a corn cutter and real thick gloves. We cut a wide path through the clump of brush. In a little while we discovered there was truly a cane mill setting on a mostly rotted stump.

We cut the bigger trees from around the cane mill with a chain saw. But there was a problem. There were trees literally growing between the mashing drums and gears. With a hand saw, we cut out what we could. After a while the mill was free of tree limbs. Daddy, Shorty, me and Gilbert Hilton hoisted it onto Uncle Shorty's pickup truck and headed for River Ridge. Well, with little more discussion or talk, I guess this venture just started off. With all the rust and extra brush, I can bet the thing weighed at least 800 pounds. The remainder of the first day was spent under the big white oak tree in the backyard with small pliers and pocket-knives. We took turns working splinters of wood from the drums and gears.

The metal drive mechanism was locked up tighter than Dick's hat band. But, this was just a minor setback facing the number of technical advisors growing by the day. Elmer wanted all of us kids to see the molasses being made, but there were also plenty of other men and women in the community who just wanted to see it done one more time. Over the next few days, weeks and months, each rusty bolt was oiled and carefully coaxed out. When possible, a shiny new bolt or part replaced the old. Everything that could be wire-brushed, cleaned and oiled was. Care was given to not get one drop of oil on the rusty mashing drums. All the bearings were rusted tight and had to be replaced. A trip to Roanoke was made just to find the expensive ancient replacement bearings. It took more than a month to find new bearing races for the gears. But they, too, were found.

In far less than two months, the molasses press was ready for a test run. With the gearbox full of new gear oil, the old thing was free and turning once again. For a week or so, everybody who came by would spin the big fly wheel and say something like, "By damn who would have thought it." Everyone in the crowd was happy with their own efforts.

As with so many things on River Ridge, Chuck Shorter was a part. Chuck plowed up about a two-acre piece of land on his farm over on the creek. One Saturday morning in May, we planted the sugar cane, and the long summer of work began. About every Saturday Daddy, me and my siblings headed for the cane field. Often other older grown men came along. We chopped weeds until the field was clean.

"Feel that sweat on your back; now that is good for you. That is the feeling of television being torn from your guts. Makes the poison come to the top and drop off'n you," said Daddy. (It is so funny how often I tell youth today that hard walking is just the television either coming out or looking for a softer place in your body.)

Daddy would tell one story after another about chopping corn over in the horseshoe on the Flanagan Farm and how the hard work was never ending. "I don't want to kill you off. I just want you to see how hard old people had to work to make a living. In your life you will do better. That is all," he said.

Shorty and once in awhile Uncle Nelson chopped weeds too. Uncle Shorty even brought "Old Ted the Horse" a time or two to bust the middles of the cane rows. I don't know if it was to help us out. I think it was for him to feel the two-footed plow in his hands and smell horse sweat and watch the earth turn over. But he came, and it was a help. Sweat dripped off the end of his nose, but he was smiling, too.

After work we would load up in Uncle Shorty's old International pickup truck. With the wind blowing through our hair and sweat drying in the air made by the moving truck, we headed off for the old store up in Norris Run. We all got a cold Double Cola, a hunk of yellow cheese and a big oatmeal cake. It was cool up there along the spring branch under the big over-hanging trees. It was fun just to set down in the cool water and eat my cheese and oatmeal cake. I might have been a little old for this kind of food, but I never let on. "Cheese cut right out of the hoop is the freshest best kind. Good, ain't it?" the old man at the store would say. I just liked it a lot.

At 60, I still do. I still remember the ride in the back of the truck, too. Not so much for the taste but for memory of going, the laughter hard work brings and thoughts of a truly simpler time in my own life.

And being with Daddy, Shorty and my family! I think the storytellers refer to it as "memories of a bygone era." Today, some of the more educated people call it some kind of male bonding. Well, it must have worked some, for most of us are still here, still friends and still eating cheese and oatmeal cakes.

Now, if you want to see something funny, show up at a Lytton family meeting with oatmeal cakes and cheese and watch how we all put the cheese in the middle of our oatmeal cake. You can set back and listen to the stories of how and when we learned to eat them this way. At this point the cheese is no longer just a noun. Cheese becomes something else—maybe even alive. Often referred to as "Them Cheese-is awful good." *Them Cheese* is a thing, a reminder of a place, a phrase used to tell time in history and a reminder of great taste.

Once the cane was planted and the old mill was turning, the next thing was getting the mill set up and cleaned. I was sent to the railroad right-of-way to look for five or six solid old crossties. Once I delivered them to the house, not just Daddy and Shorty but the whole family and even some people from the community started the process of mounting the old mill and setting it in place for crushing and squeezing cane. In the old days a wooden pole was attached to the center crank, and a horse or mule would walk in the circle all day long, pulling the pole to turn the squeezing drums.

This was not the case for us. Elmer and the other men just kept bragging on how easy this was going to be, because this mill had a very large wheel attached to a central turning shaft. You see, this rusty old thing was one of the new types of cane mills.

The power take-off on a small tractor provided power, while the tractor sat stationary. One afternoon, Chuck Shorter came over driving his old International Farmall "C" tractor. It had a power take off pulley. To this pulley we placed a wide belt that we then looped over the mill's big wheel. When the tractor was put in gear, the old mill slowly but noisily came to life. Quite possibly this was the first time it had turned like this in 50 years.

Over the next month or so we continued to hoe cane. We also searched out all old sweet corn patches in the area. The corn stalks were hauled home and run though the old mill. Some people, folks we did not even know, brought small pickup truckloads of corn to be mashed and to watch the mill work. "Yessir, I just think it is going to work," they would chuckle.

With each new stalk, more of the old rust came off the squeezing drums and corn juice ran down into a waiting bucket. With each stalk, the drums got brighter. The newly mashed stalks were fed to milk cows, and corn sap was fed to the hogs. Both seemed to like the stuff. The people from River Ridge and beyond seemed to like the whole idea of making homemade sorghum molasses, too. They would tell stories of when, as kids, they had made molasses.

As the days drew closer to starting the molasses-making, a giant pile of wood was amassed. Believe it or not, Uncle Shorty cleaned up every old lumber pile and stacks of un-burnt firewood for miles around. I even helped Mr. Cook clean out a small fence-row for the wood. A few people brought piles of old fence-posts. There was truly a mountain of wood the size of a house in the backyard. I thought to myself there was no way the old devil himself could burn up that pile of wood. Little did I know that I would be searching the world over for more wood before this project was over. But it was all worth it to hear Uncle Shorty scream and run off through a cow pasture saying, "That is it for me. There can be no less than a skillion skunks under that pile of wood. By damn, *you* go in there. I just ain't a-going." (Yes, a skillion, not a million—with skunks a different numbering system is used.)

Few people came when the actual process of cutting the cane started. But more came when the mashing of each stalk and the boiling down of the sap began. Molasses-making took on the feeling of a carnival. About 95 percent of the water in each pan of juice had to evaporate or boil away. This does take a long time. Truly, people came well before daylight and did not leave until the full pan of molasses was finished. Often we were far after midnight getting the molasses into jars. During this 18-hour job, cane was still being mashed and wood was still being brought in. Green sap was being continually skimmed off the surface of the cooking molasses. Old men appeared with moonshine, then left. Young men brought in beer and store-bought whisky and joined in the laughter and worked side by side with the more experienced molasses-makers. Breakfast, lunch, supper, another supper and a few late evening snacks came and went as the pan of juice slowly simmered its way toward molasses.

Old Mr. Harman Harry was our main advisor. He just kept telling us to keep it cooking. "You don't want to have to chase them molasses around your plate. You want them to stand up on the top of your bread." So, we cooked them and then cooked them some more and then cooked them some more. We finally just said, "Enough cooking. They have just got to be molasses." Then we carefully poured them into jars and set them aside.

The next morning when them molasses had cooled down, we thought there would be no chasing them molasses at all. They would not even come out of the jar. The next day, each jar had to warm up in a pan of hot water until them molasses liquefied again to be poured back into the new pan of simmering molasses just to thin them down some. By now, I did not worry much about chasing them molasses across a plate. I just wanted some sleep and to get on with this molasses-making. Today, I think Mr. Harry just liked being a part of something that he did back in this earlier life. He did not want this adventure to end.

News reporters even came to check out the molasses-making on River Ridge. Mother spoke to each of the reporters and smiled and posed for pictures. The picture we all liked the most was of Mom standing in front of a pile of mashed cane stalks. Bees of every description were there in masses, two or three new kinds of houseflies were circling around, and there were a few less than a million dog-pecker gnats. The pile of squeezed cane stalks was more than 20 feet tall and 50 feet wide. Mom just sat there on the growing pile and smiled and acted like the bees weren't stinging too much, like the flies were not biting, and gnats weren't flying into her ears. Uncle Lake called one afternoon to say: "Well how is the molasses making coming along? Ruth you are famous!"

Uncle Lake and Aunt Nellie lived in Hagerstown, Maryland. Lake went on to tell us that his local newspaper ran a story about Mother and molasses-making on River Ridge, Virginia. Mother was now as famous as Old Miss Kadle and known everywhere all over River Ridge, in parts of Long Shop and the upper side of McCoy; parts of Sunnyside, too, and Hagerstown, Maryland, for sure. Uncle Lake brought copies of the news article on his next trip home. Mother has them to this day. Famous people keep a lot of reminders of their fame. That way when lesser known famous people come around you have proof of your fame. Momma had hers!

We made molasses for the next two or three years, and then we just stopped. The carnival atmosphere was gone. "All of the sugar has done been licked off'n this here sucker," Elmer was heard to say. The old mill set in the backyard for a year or two, well-greased and oiled, all covered with a tarp. We often used its crossties as seats in the yard. Then one day, the rightful owners came for the cane mill. As far as I know, they set it back out in the field among the locust trees and the green briers. In no time at all, traces of making molasses were gone from the backyard. Today, I can just bet that the old mill has done rusted away and is nothing more than a brown spot on the earth.

Now, here is what I learned from molasses-making. It was very hard work, but old men revel in hard work and the memory of past molasses-making. I think that these particular old men stopped and thought about old people they once knew, too. They just took to the work and hard liquor. Old women did, too. It is the way they grew up. I think Elmer wanted me to know this.

Now that I am 60 years old I understand more of Elmer's objectives, and think back and chuckle. I also think that every person needs and should have their own personal few minutes of fame. Even today, you ask Mother about molasses-making, and she will tell you about the newspaper clipping first and about the work second. Every time I eat molasses I can see Mom setting in front of that big pile of sugar cane stalks just smiling. I see her carrying out sandwiches and pop to the workers, too.

Shucking Corn

Old people weren't always old, just like you ain't going to always be young.

WHEN I WAS JUST A KID, my family had little patches of field corn planted all over the community. Sometimes we would grow corn on the shares with landowners. You see everybody needed corn. Everybody had hogs to fatten and a milk cow, and some even had a steer they were trying feed out for beef. So everybody that could planted corn.

In the spring we plowed up land within a day's horse walk from home. Me, I have rode on old Ted's back all the way to Toms Creek or almost all the way to Prices Fork. Uncle Shorty or Daddy would walk leading Old Ted. We would plow up a small patch of ground, sometimes no bigger than two or three gardens. "Corn and beans are corn and beans," Daddy would say. Shorty and Nelson agreed. It is funny to think back today. These three men would fuss and argue all the way to the field and cuss all the way home. But, the next week they just started off almost arm-in-arm together again. They were truly family.

Each small patch was planted in corn that just seemed to tower over us. I bet it grew 10 feet tall. About every 10 feet down the corn row a bean seed was planted. The bean plants would climb almost to the top of the corn plants. About every 50 feet down the bean and corn row, a pumpkin seed was dropped. Every once in a while a green-striped cushaw seed was dropped, too. (Cushaws make a better pumpkin pie than a pumpkin does.) In the early summer you chopped the weed. By midsummer you laid the corn by. That meant the corn plants completely shaded the field and weeds had a hard time growing.

We picked pole beans from early summer to frost. A pole bean is a good-tasting bean, but they are lot of work. We would pick every bucket and tub full that we could find. For hours we set under the weeping willow tree in Mammaw's yard stringing beans. "If them college men at VPI are so smart, why in the world don't they invent a pole bean without them strings?" men would say. Everyone agreed and just laughed and keep on stringing. "They will be better than a snowball in a jar this winter," Grandmother would remind her sons.

In late fall we would go to the fields and start pulling pumpkins and cushaws. We cooked down some to can and filled the cellar with fresh ones that we could eat on all winter. We hauled some to everybody up and down River Ridge. The others we fed to the hogs and milk cows. Hog and cows loved them, too. I guess they thought they were just uncooked pumpkin pies or something.

In late fall, we sharpened up the corn cutters and headed to the field. A corn cutter is a big old knife about 24 inches long. You would grab a-holt of a stalk of the tall corn and swing the corn cutter up over your head and chop down on the stalk. The objective was to cut it off just an inch or two above the ground. You then carried all of your cut stalks to one central location and stacked them together to create a fodder shock. Once the corn stalks were cut their name changed: they were now fodder. Our small field may have ended up with no more than 15 fodder shocks. There the ears of corn continued to dry. So did the corn stalks.

When the frost got closer, it became important to start feeding more and more corn to the hogs and cattle set aside for beef. They needed to be fattened up a lot. Hog lard was the mainstay of all cooking there on River Ridge! No one truly wanted a beef steak without a big ring of white fat all the way around it. That fat was made by feeding corn and lots of it.

Here is something that I thought was funny. Even today, I still can hear the men's reaction on finding an off-colored ear of corn. Mr. Gilbert Hilton once told me that when they were teenagers some of the farmers would host corn shucking parties. On a bright moonlit night with just a hint of frost in the air, young men and women with courting on their mind would come to the corn shucking. Out in the middle of the field people built a large bonfire and made hot chocolate for the event. Girls often brought warm cakes and pies.

Well, one fodder shock after another was dragged to the light of the fire. Boys and girls alike stood on their knees and started shucking corn. If you just happened to shuck an ear of corn that was not truly yellow like the others, you got to kiss the girl closest to you. If you just happened upon a red ear of corn, you got to kiss the prettiest girl at the corn shucking. Often a real good red ear of corn was held onto from year to year.

As we shucked corn, some of the stories told about these nights would make me blush. I can remember Uncle Lake shucking off a colored ear of corn and asking, "I wonder what ever happened to Evelyn Walker? She sure was a pretty thing on them frosty nights. You had to have a blood-red ear just to have been able set and eat her pies. She lives the other side of Blacksburg these days, and no one sees her too much. She's got a house full of about-grown kids and a flush toilet, too."

Another thing funny was the girls and boys named in these stories. Today, the ones I know of are old prim and proper people and would just never do the things that Mod and Daddy laughed about. Daddy laughed and said to me, "We wasn't always old." Uncle Fred said, "Well, just how in hell do you think you got here?"

An Interesting Drink

THROUGHOUT THIS GROUPING of stories I have talked about my uncles' and father's drinking habits. I have to tell you about one of the funniest mixed drinks I ever experienced. Yes, experience is truly what it was. Who were the participants? Chuck Shorter and Waitsie Winters for two, me for three. There were others, but their names have slipped into the last 45 years. I do not recall how it arrived or from where it came, but all of a sudden we were the owners of a brand new, never-been-opened, half gallon of store-bought vodka. The good stuff; it still had the label on the bottle and everything. Its origin is still a mystery. It is not relevant to the story anyway.

What I do remember is that we took the bottle to Chuck's log cabin on the farm. Waitsie was older and knew how to properly mix vodka into a good mixed drink. You know, kind of like town boys do. After this day I would forever question his knowledge and skills related to alcohol. Chuck rummaged through the cabin and found up a package of "Leftie Lemon." In my day, everyone drank Kool Aid. Lefty Lemon was a knock-off version of Kool Aid.

Chuck finds the Lefty Lemon and a gallon jar. He goes to the creek and gets about a half gallon of water. Then he pours the Lefty Lemon into the jar. Waitsie then stirs in about a pound or more of sugar. Once the Lefty Lemon and sugar are dissolved,

123

Waitsie slowly stirs in the vodka. When the gallon jar is about full, a small sip of this wonderful concoction is poured for us to taste.

The mixture is so sweet it is sickening. You are supposed to get sick the day after you drink the stuff, not when you taste it. Everyone starts to look at Chuck and Waitsie with a very discriminating eye. They start to review the recipe and the mixture. It is discovered the "Leftie Lemon" is the pre-sweetened kind. The mixture has been double sweetened. There is nothing to do but sour it back up. Chuck goes to the cabinet and brings out a bottle of apple cider vinegar. They start adding in a little vinegar, and slowly but surely the mixture becomes sourer. Everyone gets a glass full.

Now to be quite honest here, I was grateful for the vodka; well I think I was. Everyone had a great laugh at the look of Chuck's face when the mistake was discovered. But there was still a very funny taste about this mixed drink. My advice to you novice mixers is: do not to use creek water or just any old jar from the sideboard. Rinse the jar out a few times. Another thing: there is a big difference between creek water and cold branch water!

Little Brown Bottles

Sometimes the little things mean more to other people
than you ever know. So always be real careful whose
things you go and run down.

WELL, THE TRUTH IS I once had two little brown
bottles. When I got big enough to walk into the
liquor store and buy a bottle of liquor like a regular
Appalachian American, I was happier than a puppy
with two peters. Truly there were at least 100 kinds,
but I had had my eye on a little brown jug of bourbon.
I liked the shape and price. Cheap was always a major
factor in everything I ever did. It just seemed like I
never had two brown pennies to rub together. But I did
have my little brown jug. It just fit perfectly in the glove
box in my little blue and white pickup truck. I chose to
refill the little brown jug with whatever was cheap.

All went well for a few months, until one day I
caught Daddy, Nelson, Buck, Mr. Luther and Gilbert
Hilton out at the truck. They literally drank the bottle
dry! I had to change over to Scotch after Daddy and
the other men got to drinking it. Turnabout is fair
play, but expensive. I had been sneaking around and
drinking up their hooch for years. But, I did get the
best of them! I started to refill the little brown jug with
real cheap Scotch, which they would only drink as a
last resort. They would cuss a while, but drink it down.

125

"Why in the whole big world does he want to drink up something as bad as that stuff?" the men would say. They never learned that you have got to cut Scotch with a Grapette, and I never told it to them either.

That little brown jug was really important to me. In my own mind it was like I was now a full-grown Appalachian American: I carried my alcohol in my own bottle! I was like most of the other men on The Ridge. Thankfully that phase only lasted a year or so. But I was to learn the importance of a second little brown bottle.

One day, I was up in Saw Mill Holler squirrel hunting. The season would be coming in soon, and I always liked to have a little jump on the other hunters, so I chose to open my hunting season before The Great State of Virginia did theirs. Well, it was a right warm August morning, and I had not brought anything for the gnats and flies or any water for me. So I worked my way down into the holler and raked the leaves off of a small spring branch. I dug out a hole in the mud just below the cinder block spring box and set down to wait for the water to clear up. I set down first; then I lay down. If I was going to take a nap I needed something to rest my head on, so I looked around a little. My hand came to rest on a little brown bottle. I just pushed it up under my head and took a very good nap right out there in the woods down deep in Saw Mill Holler with nothing going through my head but the trickle of water and the clear blue sky over head.

When I woke up I had a very nice pool of cool, clean spring water. I lay down on my belly in the thick oak and hickory leaves and skimmed off the little water bugs and spiders and the blue sky's reflection wiggled in the water. I drank my fill of nature's coolest and purest water. Mountain water is the best kind there is! And there is no worry of its purity either. All my life I have been told that water needs to flow over three rocks to be clean and pure. There sure were more than that in Saw Mill Hollow.

Holy Macaroni, life is just great, ain't it? I got almost to the railroad and thought it might be a good idea to take a cool drink of water with me. So I walked over to where I had taken my nap and picked up the little brown bottle and a small stick. I took to digging out the rotten leaves and dirt. It took a good ten minutes to remove the trash from out of the bottle. I rinsed it clean with the pure water and filled it full with nature's best! I started down the railroad track for home, sipping on my spring water, and for some reason I stopped to look at the bottle. It was an old antique brown Coke bottle. Not one chip or crack. I had never seen one before. I stuck it in my backpack with my dead squirrels, and when I got home I showed the squirrels and the old Coke bottle to Daddy.

He was so caught up on the bottle that he almost didn't see my sack of fresh squirrels. I cleaned and dressed the squirrels and he went in the house to clean up the old bottle. Mother Ruth came out and asked me what had gotten Elmer in such a cleaning uproar. Daddy said that when he was little boy he carried water and drinks to the men cutting the oak and hickory timber out of the big holler. Just below the spring box there once stood and operated a big saw mill. "You never know. I might have carried this here bottle down the railroad tracks and into the holler for someone to drink," he said.

The little brown Coke bottle was of no value to

me, so I gave it to Daddy. He kept it in his sock drawer where it would not get chipped or broken. I never saw him take it out of the sock drawer. About this time, I left River Ridge for the University of Rhode Island, and also along about then Daddy started having all of his leg and knee problems. The arthritis got so bad that he had to stop work, and unbeknownst to me, times got real hard for Mother and Daddy.

When I came home from the University of Rhode Island, with tears in his eyes, Daddy told me of their misfortunes and he said that he had to sell the Coke bottle while I was off at school. He sold the bottle to a local antique dealer for $17.00. They needed money. Later, I saw the bottle on the store shelf, but the dealer would not sell it back to me. He said it was not for sale. I tried to explain just how much it meant to Daddy. The owner just said, "I am truly sorry; but Elmer will just have to get over it." Daddy did and I did.

I had not seen another old Coke bottle in years. Then one day I was walking through an antique shop in Charlottesville and there was a shelf of more than ten of them. I just looked at them. Elmer has passed on and is over it, too. But, back in 1980, if I had seen those bottles, I would have purchased two of them: one for Elmer and one for me.

What's a Body
To Do?

The Same House,
But There Was No Ham!

At a manager's meeting one of the owners of the Mick or Mack Store told the group, "Words are free, but I want work."

I HAVE LITTLE STORIES ABOUT and some experience in many of the same places my father and other family members described. For example, it is the first day of squirrel season. I find myself back in the neck of the woods where Daddy and I delivered a cooked ham to this house a few years before. It is way before daylight when the urge hits me to go to the bathroom. I check my pockets, and I have no striking paper. It is darker than that little inside room off of Grandmother's closet where she keeps the Christmas packages hidden. I try to look for a soft mullein weed, but I cannot find one. Mullein weeds are the best of all the weeds to use for toilet paper when the urge hits, if you know what I mean.

There is nothing to do but walk out the path to the nearest house for a toilet. I mean an outside toilet. You see, everyone had an outside toilet, and they were right easy to find. You did not need no flashlight, either. You just were kind of drawn toward any house, and you just kind of got led toward the

131

toilet, if you are catching my drift here.

Well, without a light, I am drawn to this unfamiliar seat of ease. It is still very dark, but morning is coming fast. On the eastern mountain there is a blue line forming, but birds are not singing much as yet. They will be waking up in just a few minutes, and the squirrels will be waking up, too. I drop my drawers and set down.

I reckon that I have been seated maybe one minute, when all of a sudden the toilet door swings open and in steps the lady of the house. She screams real loud like a wildcat and just runs out of the toilet. I let out some kind of sick animal call. I am so scared that in less than a second I loudly empty the contents of my bowels.

I go to the house to try to apologize for scaring the poor old lady. She just kind of looks at me and says nothing. So I pick up my trusty Old Springfield and fade back into the safety of the woods, and as the last stars vanish morning gets itself started again. Before me the woods just seem to come alive, and I am grateful just to be there, just me and a trusty 12-gauge.

I found myself lighter and wiser too. Yes, I truly had the stuffings scared right out of me. I think that lady might have passed a little gas too, but I could not tell. I was much too mannerly a little boy to have asked her. She might have needed to check her drawers, too. That always keeps a person from wanting to talk.

Oh Yes, He Did Poop in His Britches

A FEW YEARS BACK I took this little boy to summer camp. He was just like any of the other hundreds of little boys I had taken to camp over the years. About the only difference was he had never once been away from home. I mean he had never, *ever* been away from home in his whole 11 years of life. Oh, he had been to the store with his parents, walked the mountains squirrel-hunting with older brothers and even gone to the river once or twice. His mother did say that a year or so back he had gone to his grandmother's one time, but he would not spend the night. His grandmother lived across the gravel road from his house. She had to walk him home before supper.

Petey's mother said: "It was just too much aggravation putting up with his homesickness, so we always left him here at the house." When she called me one day and told me the whole story, she said, "Mr. Lytton, do you think he could go to summer camp with you this summer?"

"Sure, Petey can go with me. Why, we are buddies! I see him often at school. A few of his friends are going, too."

"Are you sure? You know how he is kind of backwards and ain't going to want to go anywhere. He just will not leave the house except for school and that is it. He is lazy, too. He will watch a very bad TV show rather than get up and change the channel. I think going to summer camp with you would be real good for Petey," said his mom.

The morning for loading up the bus for summer camp finally came. Petey and his mom were right on time. They got in the check-in line just like everyone else, and everything went off without a hitch. Now, Petey would not ride the bus, so he climbed into my pickup truck, and we followed the bus to the camp. I found him to be a very nice and happy young fellow. We laughed and told fishing and hunting stories all the way to camp. I was starting to think that this "need to be at home by dark" issue that his mother and I had discussed was a thing of the past. I was even thinking that I had totally misunderstood his mother. We laughed and joked all the way to camp. When we arrived, Petey moved in like all the other kids.

About 5:30 p.m. just before supper, I walked past my pickup truck and saw Petey's luggage in the back. On the way to dinner I met up with Petey and asked him, "Why is your luggage back in my truck?"

"Well, it will soon be dark, and I need to go back to my house," he said very matter-of-fact-like.

"Now, Petey, your mom and dad have purchased you a week of camp."

"I just need to go home real quick; I just need to go home." He was not upset or irritated at all. For him it was just a simple fact that it was time to be heading for home.

"Come on over here to my truck. I have one of

those new cellular telephone devices here in the back. We will just call your mom and let her tell us what to do. Is that fair enough?" I asked.

"Yes, Mom will be coming as soon as we call her," Petey said confidently.

We dug out the bag phone. Petey showed me how he set the antenna out on the car hood of his dad's car. He explained how he always placed a small piece of cloth under the magnet so the car's paint would not get scratched. We set the bag phone down on the seat of my truck, and Petey dialed his mother's telephone number. Right then, one of my co-workers started walking toward my truck. She just was checking out all of the commotion with the telephone and calling. When Petey's mother, Mrs. Gilroy, answered, Petey said "hello" and told her that I needed to talk with her. I told her that he had loaded his luggage in my truck and truly wished to come home.

Mrs. Gilroy asked if he was sick or anything.

"No, old Petey is happy and fine; he just wants to be back on Buckhorn Mountain with you and his dad. What are your wishes?" I asked.

"Well, if he is ok, I would like for him to stay at least one night. Can you manage that?"

"Sure, but I want you to tell him he is staying."

I handed the telephone back to Petey, and Mrs. Gilroy told him she would not be coming to pick him up, because she wanted him to stay the night.

Petey took to shaking all over like a real sick dog and kind of mumbling in some unknown language. It may have been a lost version of Navaho that has not been spoken in more than a thousand years. My co-worker and I did not know that Petey was bilingual. All of a sudden, I hear this low guttural sound, and it isn't his voice I am hearing. Then there was a much louder sound, and Petey's face turned an ashen white and he started to sweat. Judging by the noise and smell I knew what he had done. My co-worker's eyes got real big, and she quickly walked away. Petey just handed me the telephone. I told Mrs. Gilroy of the big sounds, smell and sweat. I explained what I thought just happened, and she broke out in uncontrolled laughter. I told her that we would call back in a little while. When Petey handed me the telephone, he had turned around and grabbed his butt with his hand and looked at me like a stillborn calf. I guess he wanted to keep the contents of his shorts out of his shoes or something.

When I carefully walked him the back way to the cabin, he took great care with each and every step. I asked him to strip down outside on the grass and quickly take a good shower with lots of soap! When I looked down at the soiled clothes before me, I almost got sick on my stomach. I had no clue that there was that much stuff up in a small boy. Trying to figure out what to do with the clothes was a problem. While I was leaning in the fork of a red oak retching, I saw a real strong stick. I used it to pick up—oh so carefully— each piece of clothing and pitched them as far into the woods as I could. As for me, I wasn't touching or washing them rascals! I was already sick enough. Let Mother Nature do with them whatever she wanted.

In a little while, Petey was showered and had on a new set of clothes. He had on a lot of that Jade East cologne, too; so he still smelled, but it was a much more tolerable aroma. We called Mrs. Gilroy. I just handed the telephone to Petey. The first thing he said was, "You will not believe what you made me do, and Mr. Lytton pitched my good shirt and britches into the woods with a stick. Mommy, please stop laughing! I want you to come and get me and take me home."

I took the telephone and told her "Everything he says is true. Now what is our plan?"

"I would like for him to stay."

"Well, I don't think there is enough stuff up in Petey for that to happen again ever," I said. Then I looked at Petey and said, "You are staying, so you need to get your suitcase and move back into the cabin. Petey stayed the whole week. By day he had loads fun and even tried his hand at dancing a time or two. By evening he just sat close to me. His mom picked him on Friday, and all was well with the world.

Petey never came back to camp. But every time I saw him he had a look of terror on his face. I just knew that he was hoping that I would not tell our little secret. He is now about 35 years old and is employed by an engineering firm near Charlotte, North Carolina. He comes to town once or twice a year. Each time he stops by my office. Me, I have never told a soul of this night until now. Petey's two children are regulars at camp. Neither have had one minute's problem being away from home. Once I heard Petey and his wife tell their children, "If you have any trouble, find Mr. Lytton. He will take care of you; he always took care of us." Well Petey, I will always try to do my best; just like I did with you! But every time I see you I just kind of hear those loud stomach sounds.

Very Bad Gas,
and Some Flatulence, Too

I NEVER MET A COUNTRY BOY who was not aware of the importance of having strong gas. Some might tell you the human body produces gas as part of the digestive process and is a healthy thing. I do not think that this true at all. I think the body, especially the human Appalachian male's body, produces loud, smelly flatulence more for the humor of it than for any health-related reasons.

One of the most powerful farting experiences of my life, my whole life I mean, maybe in anybody's life, was led by none other than my particular friend Chuck Shorter. We were both in high school and members of the track team. Chuck was the school bus driver, and we had gotten ourselves all loaded up to head to Narrows to a track meet. Chuck had also gotten his jaw loaded up with chewing tobacco, and had it munched up pretty good. Were getting ready to leave, so Chuck let out a spit glob. Around the corner came Cam Wiley. He was the track coach. Chuck did not see him coming around the end of the bus, and Mr. Wiley did not see the spit glob coming either. It was about the size of croquet ball, and it made the door at the same time Mr. Wiley did. Cam was fast, I mean fast. He managed to get his clipboard up and knocked the spit down like it was a softball. "Damn you, Chuck Shorter, I ort to kick your ass" was all he said. That was right funny, because he was about half the size of Chuck Shorter. Holy Macaroni, he was a good person and a fine teacher.

After that I kind of expected that this was going to be a good trip. It was off to a good start anyway. Anything that started off with good cussing, lots of laughter and good friendship was going to be good. But we kind of knew that great humor was now over. All the way over and back, Chuck farted some bad ones. I might have let a few myself, but nothing like what he was generating. On the way home, Mr. Wiley and I were setting in the seat just behind the driver's seat. That would be Chuck's seat. All of a sudden I saw Chuck kind of wiggle and scratch his head and screw his hat down tight. I had all too often seen this gesture, and was well aware of what was coming. I do honestly think that he, too, was surprised by what came next.

This gust of flatulence came flying over the seat and kept going. That fart had handles and took a-holt and would not turn loose. When the odor hit me, I stuck my head out the bus window. Windows started coming open and sounded like dominos being knocked over. Mr. Wiley stuck his head out beside me and said, "You damn fart-mocker, why did you do that? You might have shit on me. And get the hell out of that window, I need a little air in here."

To this day, I bet you that Mr. Wiley thinks that I farted right on him, but I didn't. Only Chuck Shorter was capable of such a powerful and boastful thing. I was truly scared to get around Chuck for a while. I did think that he needed to shake his britches or at least scrape them out! I can just bet if any of those on that bus in 1968 read this they will say, "I do remember that afternoon! Holly Macaroni, it was strong.

There Is Your Good Pee
and There Is Bad Pee, Too

BEING A GOOD PEE-ER is not always a bad
thing. In the mid-1980s, I am working on the farm
at Whitethorn. I am running an old Allis Chalmers
Gleaner combine up and down the field. I am in hog
heaven and having the time of my life! As a child I once
dreamed that I would have the chance to do things
like drive an old combine. As the expression goes, it
just does not get any better than this. But things can
go wrong real quick.

Corn is ripe and dry. The old thrash box is
shaking all over, and the wore-out combine has about
a thousand sounds that are unique to its operation.
Corn dust is so thick in the air that I cannot see much
beyond the front of the machine. After a few days
you just get used to the sounds, smells, motions and
dust. You get to the point that all you can see is the
corn vanishing into the machine's belly and shell corn
growing in the corn bin behind your head. Golly, it is
a great day! You start to learn that each motion of the
machine has its own sounds.

Up until now the old thing is just humming,
moving much like a ballet dancer. I say to myself,

141

"Now what is that new sound?" I stop and look the old combine over. I grease each and every bearing again just to make sure that I had not overlooked one earlier in the day. I sweep off the thick layer of dust that has accumulated on the machine. I start back to shelling corn.

There it is again. I hear this high-pitched sound of something just not right. I stop and take a little broom and sweep off the dust and dirt again. The belts look ok; the chains are ok, too. I think that I should just stop shelling corn and drive the combine to the farm shop and look the thing over. Possibly, Chuck can find this new squeak. When I turn off the corn-shelling component, the squeak quiets, so I let the old thing cool off a little more. Again, I search for this new problem. No luck. So after few minutes I head for the shop. I have not gone more than 100 yards when the noise gets louder and more intense. I stop! It is time for more help. Now I smell smoke. I step out of the combine cab, and I see smoke from a bearing on the side of the machine.

I get to thinking: I need to cool this situation before the machine catches on fire. I have no water jug or fire extinguisher. You guessed it! Being an experienced pee-er like I am, I just pee on it. The smoke stops. In a few minutes, it starts to smoke some more, so I dig deep in me and pee some more.

I think that old combine saw me as an equal adversary. I bet it said to itself, "I might as well quit smoking. If I don't, he will just pee on me some more. This boy is plum full of pee."

When we worked on the old thing, all I could think was, "This thing smells like old pee!"

142

Remembering
Old Country
Stores

The Old Store and
The Fight of the Day

FAMILY AND FRIENDS have asked me more than once about the old store and why I went there every evening. I like to say I went to the store for the education, local color and honest-to-goodness indoctrination into the world. Ready or not, that same world that someday I would have to step right into. There was always someone willing to share a story about some prank they pulled long ago. A long story about different people that lived up and down the creek was always in the air.

Actually, there were two stores in Long Shop. It seems like I like to tell about Tom Long's Store a lot. The other local store was Gallimore's Store. The old store building is still there, but it has two apartments in it now.

Mr. Gallimore and his wife ran the store. A lot of people called Mr. Gallimore "Fountain Pen." He was truly one of the smallest men I knew. By the time I was eleven or twelve, I was taller than he was. His old store had mostly canned food and clothes. He carried the old men's work clothes and brogan shoes. We bought very little there. One thing that I remember

145

about Fountain Pen is each time I went into the store he'd say: "I bet you can't drink a Double Cola bottle full."

Well, after some practice I finally got to where I could drink the whole pint without putting the bottle down. I guess it took me 30 bottles of pop to get tough enough to drink the full bottle. Then he said, "That is good, real good, now drink it full." He thought that was real funny. My eyes and throat just burned. I got a piece of Mary Jane candy there one time that was so hard that it almost pulled out my teeth to eat it. He smiled at me and said, "I am glad to see you try that candy. It has been a long time since anyone bought one of those." Some of the stuff just stayed on the shelf for many years!

Another thing about Mr. Gallimore was his smell. He never put on any aftershave lotion or deodorant. He said that he just dabbed on a little vanilla extract behind his ears each day. Well, there were a few other parts that needed more than a little vanilla.

Another thing about the store, it did not have set hours. Mr. Gallimore opened when he got ready, and he went home when he got ready. He demonstrated true Appalachian Independence. I liked that, unless I wanted something.

It was on the porch of the Gallimore Store that I watched my first real fist fight. I had never seen anything like it in my whole life. Moviemaker Cecil B. DeMille could not have scripted it any better.

There were lots of families that lived in and around Long Shop, McCoy and Toms Creek that did not get along. Every once in a while, one family would get mad at members of one of the other families. A really small feud would start. There would be an argument, rarely a fistfight, and soon everything would be over. But this one had been brewing for a few weeks. (I am not going to mention any names here. Some of these men still live in this neck of the woods, and you never know who is listening.)

Anyway, this fight had been looming for a few weeks, and on the day things were coming to a head everybody knew it. I bought me up a large Double Cola—it was bigger than either Coke or Pepsi and I might have needed the larger one to get through this. I went out on the store porch and picked me one of the better-looking carbide cans for a set. The two fellas involved looked like men to me, even though they were not more than 16 or 17 years old.

When the fight began, the families started yelling encouragement to their brother and real rough obscenities at their brother's foe. Everybody was screaming and pushing. In the beginning, I truly thought that both families were going to jump in and start a big-time brawl, which would have been my first. But they did not. Only one of the fighters' older brothers did jump in and punch the other fighter in the face a few times. Then he quickly retreated, when it looked like one of the others were coming for him. In reality the whole fight lasted no more than a few minutes.

When it was over, both fighters came up and leaned on the store porch. Their noses were bleeding; they both had big knots on their heads and puffy eyes. Both had blood around their teeth. One of the combatants said, "Harmie, can I have a drink of that Double Cola?"

"Hell yes, drink all you want," I said.

Both families kept hollering obscenities at each other and informing others that "this ain't over yet." But you could look into the fighters' eyes and see that it was over. There was no winner to this battle.

Yes, you go the store for an education. I learned that there is no winner in battles like this one. From the start, I do not think the two fighters liked each other, but they were not into this fight at all. I think that their families egged this on, and both lost big time. As for me. I have never wanted to watch another fight. Unless forced to fight for my personal safety or that of my family, I think I will always be able to walk away. Well, leastways, I always have!

No, I Have Never Been to the Zoo, But I Have Seen a Monkey

JUST THE OTHER DAY one of the young people I have the privilege of working with asked me, "Mr. Lytton, have you ever been to the zoo"?

I felt right unworthy when I answered her, "No I have not, but I have seen a monkey."

She looked at me right crazy like; I guess about everyone has been to a real zoo. I went on to tell her that I had even read an article in the *National Geographic* about people in Africa hunting and killing monkeys and apes for food. They called it "bush meat" or something like that. My monkey-viewing took place at Turk's Store right here in Montgomery County, Virginia, not over in Africa. These animals were far too skinny to make even jungle gravy out of, much less bush meat.

In his store, Mr. Turk had about everything one could ever want. He had shotguns and rifles, work clothes, bullets, brogan shoes, canned food and even glass jars of vegetables that local people had canned. He sold gas and beer, too. But none of these things took the Lytton Clan to the store, no sir. What took us there was pure, honest-to-goodness, clear white moonshine licker.

I'm pretty sure it wasn't made there; I think Mr. Turk just sold it. I always thought it was funny to see grown men buy a quart or a half gallon and then set about testing it for its purity. To do this you put two or three tablespoons out on the jar lid and set it on fire. If it burned blue, it was pure moonshine, and they would purchase the jar. If the flame did not burn bright blue it was not pure. Oh, it was still purchased and referred to as "old head bust." For the life of me though, I never saw moonshine ever burn any color but blue. At about eight or nine years old, I kind of dreaded having to someday drink anything that you had to set on fire to bring out the goodness in it.

Anytime I heard that Daddy, Shorty or anyone of them was going to Turk's for some beer or moonshine, I jumped into the truck. If the cab of the truck was full, I just jumped in the back. It was kind of like riding in a convertible. Mother and Mamaw were constantly reminding me that riding with the men when they were lightheaded was not good for my health, but I still went every time the truck left the property. Now, I have a question here: if they were so worried about me, why did Mom and Grandmother let me go? This was no place for an eight-year-old and hardly a place for someone 80 or 90, for that matter.

I was not going for the moonshine; I was going to see the monkeys. As soon as we arrived, I ran for a big wooden block that sat in the front of the store. I would perch myself there to watch them monkeys run. Daddy or Shorty would always bring me a seven-ounce Coke and a big nickel bag of peanuts. They'd hold the bottle while I poured the peanuts into my Coke. Now I was set to watch them monkeys.

You see, Mr. Turk had a wire cage that went almost all the way around his store, and in it lived four or five monkeys. They were maybe two times the size of a fox squirrel. They may have been small, but they were monkeys all the same, and for me that is what mattered. Sometimes they would just run around the cage real fast and holler loud enough to wake up the dead. Other times they would just sit and look at me with their lips rolled up, showing me their dirty teeth. One thing they always did was stink. You could smell them before you could see them. If there was ever an animal that needed a bath, it was Mr. Turk's monkeys. Once in awhile, they would go to the bathroom in their hand and rub the crap on the wire cage. That monkey crap was so powerful weeds would not grow under their cages; where their feces accumulated there was just bare earth. Mr. Turk never cleaned up the monkey crap and pitched it on his garden.

Their hair was real bad, too. In some places they did not have any hair at all, and in some places the hair was all matted up in knots. Uncle Shorty said they needed to be wormed and told me not to get too close or I might have to be wormed when we got home. Now I had seen Shorty worm dogs and cats, hogs and the like. I did not want a real big pill, one the size of a buck marble, pushed down my throat all the way past my tonsils. Especially, I did not want Uncle Shorty's dirty hand gouging that pill down my throat. So I gave them monkeys lots of room.

On one moonshine run when Shorty's old green International rolled to almost a stop, I broke and ran to see the monkeys only to be told that I was a week or two late. The man told me that monkeys' pee was such powerful stuff it had eaten a hole in the wire and all of the monkeys had escaped. Uncle Nelson said, "I reckon they were headed for Africa or to someplace warm."

Sometime later we learned that two of them had gotten lost on their way back to Africa and ended up in Long Shop. The rascals were living in the trees behind Pride Arrington's house and the Amos house, there just along the short bluff near the creek. As I was headed through the field behind Pride's house to the creek, I was not far from the big spring when I saw the monkeys in the trees. They still were very shaggy, and they ran very fast.

It was not long before I heard that a local man had shot them. Everybody's got to eat. I know that at my house, if you ran across something and it did not bite you too bad or have real big stickers, it got eaten. When the monkeys got shot, I just thought back to the *National Geographic Magazine* where they talked about bush meat. I guess this was bush meat Long Shop style. Daddy said this man just shot the monkeys for the sport of it. I'd never really thought about that before. Daddy said anyway they would have had a really hard time come winter. I guess someone may have just had the need to shoot something, and them monkeys came along at the wrong time. Sport shooting was new to me.

Sadly, there just isn't anyone left to ask except Momma Ruth, so one day when I went to the nursing home for a visit, I asked her about the runaway monkeys. She said that this man, whose name I am not going to mention, went down to the creek and shot the monkeys for the fun of it. Momma said he was just evil and lots of folks gave him lots of room. "Think back," she said, "your daddy and me just turned you loose to go wherever you wanted, but never in the direction of his house. He was just mean and evil."

Well, now I know who shot the monkeys, and so do you if you just think a little bit.

Morey Long and Mr. Cook and the Bull Story as Told at the Store

Grandmother once told me, "In life, no one falls up a hill. You got to work to get there."

I CAME TO TOM LONG'S Store one hot summer afternoon and found both Harman Cook and Morey Long setting on the carbide cans on opposite sides of the porch. Now, these men were certainly not strangers to the old store. In fact, you could say they were real regular customers. They just almost never came in the afternoon. You see, they were farmers and had more important things to be doing in the afternoon than to be setting around and talking, telling stories in the cool shade of the porch overhang.

But here they sat. Mr. Cook was, I guess, 75 or maybe 80 years old, and Mr. Morey Long was about the same age, maybe a day or two younger. It is safe to say they both were old enough to vote and buy beer. They were real good friends, too. They shared in each other's labor on their farms and shared farm equipment. But today, they were not setting close to one another. In fact, every once in while they would say kind of coarse words to one another. Mr. Tom Long, the store owner, said they were right irritated with each other.

154

You see, Mr. Cook had a large red bull who was given to roaming a lot. "If'n there is a cow in heat within five miles, he is going to know about it and go find her," said Mr. Cook.

When the bull got out, you had to go find him and drive him home again and fix the fence better than it was before. Sometimes this was a lot easier said than done. Often the old bull still had courting on his mind. Sometimes he still had his upper lip all rolled up. He just did not want to leave the company of a fair heifer. According the story as I was told, much earlier this morning the old men had found the hole in the fence and started after the bull. It had been easy enough to find the big rascal; he had made his way more than mile from his home pasture. They started to walk him out back toward the farm in Long Shop, and when they got to the hole in the fence, the sorry rascal balked. He wasn't going any farther. He would take off running back where they'd come from, and the old men would have to turn around and go get him again.

This had happened more than once, and everyone was about give out. On the last trip, the bull was standing almost in the hole in the fence when he just stopped and started to back up one more time. Mr. Long had picked up a big rock about the size of large potato and hit the bull in the butt as hard as he could. The rock glanced off the bull's butt and hit Mr. Cook right in the front of his head. The bull took off for Wake Forest yet again, and Mr. Cook fell to the ground like he had been shot. Then he set up and said, "Damn you, Morey, you have done kilt me this time, with your big rock; you have done kilt me for sure with your big rock!"

155

Somehow they staggered to the store for a Pepsi Cola and to recuperate. In a little while, Mr. Cook's pump knot was not so big, and his cap could once again be worn. The two old men got up and started for Wake Forest yet again. I think they captured the old bull this time. Well, I hope so any way.

Haunted House

It ain't the dead you got to keep your eye out for; it is the living. The dead has done, done all the meanness they come here to do.

As a young child, I was truly scared of ghosts. Grandmother went out of her way to make sure you were scared of the dark, scared of the man that might just come and carry you off and scared of ghosts.

When I would stay too long at Grandmother's house, she would start off telling about all the old people that once lived along the River and the Ridge. She'd get real serious about their lives and how they had died. It was pure fact that every once in a while people would still see them. It was like there was something missing in their new spiritual existence. They just came back not as real people. They must have been real enough anyways, since they came back to the Ridge just wanting to finish what they had started. Some came back to keep an eye on their old place. Other spirits came back to get even with those people that had done them wrong. They were the ghosts, and you had better always have your eye open for them! Others were just wandering souls looking for the way out. By ginkgos, come dark I was not going to show any spirit the way to the other world. Hell, I did not know where the path was, and I was not holding

157

the flashlight while we looked. I did not even know how to get to Blacksburg. So I took myself home! The ghosts could just go anywhere they wanted as long as I was safely behind them four cinder-block walls.

As I looked around River Ridge and other close communities, I realized they, too, believed in ghosts. Some of the homes had dogwood crosses over the front and back doors. Some people even nailed up very small dogwood crosses over the bedroom doors. Now these folks were not taking any chances with ghosts. At my house on River Ridge there were no dogwood crosses on any door. I guess we just trusted them ghosts would not come in. We were too poor for a ghost to have any interest anyway.

Mr. Leonard Jones lived halfway between Prices Fork and River Ridge. I would sometimes lollygag trying to catch a ride just to keep from having to walk past the Jones' house. Mr. Jones lived all alone in the two-story old rundown place. There was no grass in his yard, and he always was setting in a big rocking chair on top of a picnic table. He wore a pair of bibbed overalls that were a little dirty and far too big. There was an overgrown pond just across the fence to the side of the house. The pond was almost in his yard. Mr. Leonard Jones just set there whittling on a pointed stick. He did not talk much, but he would ask, "Where are you going or where you been?" He almost never looked up. Gilbert Hilton was a close neighbor. I ask Mr. Hilton about Leonard Jones, and about all he would say is: "He is ok; maybe a just a little possessed." I interpreted that to mean don't go near the place.

And I didn't, until I was a little older, and then

I would sneak up on the place from the back and eat grapes and peaches. If I went past on the road, though, I was running as fast as my fat little legs would carry me. I had heard Grandmother talk about such places and wasn't going to take an undue risk!

By the time I was 10 years old I was captivated by going to the stores in Long Shop. I could set on those old carbide cans as long as the doors were open. I just loved the tales the old men told. I said to the group, "In all of the stories the ghosts were people that lived long ago. Are there no new ghosts being made these days?"

The old fellows just looked from one to another and did not say a word. The place got as quiet as a graveyard, and then at last Raymond Cook spoke up: "Well, there are ghosts being made today just like in the past. It is just that people don't like to think about such things these days, or they just don't believe. Here is what I mean. Not more than two months ago we had a very bad thunderstorm, and all the power was knocked out."

With a small pause he took a drink of his Pepsi Cola and went on, "You all remember that it was dark everywhere? Well, right up the hill not far from where we set, a telephone transformer exploded and wires fell all over the ground. As it would happen Billy "Oak" Obenchain and his wife had gone to town to get coffee, sugar and some other groceries. They left their oldest daughter Loretta Obenchain home alone while they were gone."

All of the men in the store said, "This is right," and shook their heads in agreement with Mr. Cook.

He went on: "Well, about an hour before dark, when the lights went out and when the wind hard rain whistled up over the hill, Young Miss Loretta took to her bed and covered her head with lots of quilts. She was real scared. She had heard all the stories about evenings like this one. In the past when things like this happened, she had always called on her grandfather, her 'Papa,' but he had been dead for more than a year. As she lay in the bed, the telephone down in kitchen just kept ringing and popping and buzzing. Each sound the telephone made, the more scared she got.

"It was coal dark now, kind of like being in the bottom of a coal mine. Terrified and shaking real bad, Little Miss Loretta made her way down the stairs to the kitchen. When she looked out the window, she could not see any car lights and no house lights either."

My eyes looked like the bottoms of two big Pepsi Cola bottles, and I was hanging on every word.

"The old telephone on the wall rang once and then once more. She jumped, and out of habit she picked up the receiver and said, 'Hello.' And she heard a very hoarse and weak voice she knew. 'Don't you go and be scared now, Baby Girl, I am going to take care of you!' Miss Loretta pitched the telephone down and ran back up the stairs. No one ever called her 'Baby Girl' but her Grandpapa, and she knew he was dead. Not long ago she had cried over his fresh-dug grave.

"The telephone rang again and again. Slowly she went down the stairs a second time. She picked up the receiver and again the voice said, 'Don't be scared, Baby Girl. I am right here with you.' Soon she realized it really was old dead granddaddy calling her from the grave.

"Not long afterwards, the lights came back on, and the dial tone on the telephone came back too. Soon, Oak Obenchain and the rest of the family returned home. They found Miss Loretta as calm as if nothing had happened. The family members just looked back and forth at one another. They were scared to death. Just why in world wasn't Loretta?

"The next day people who shared the telephone party line came over to check on things. They explained that they had heard strange sounds on their telephone last night. 'When the power goes off, don't the telephone go off, too?' Loretta asked her father to take her to the cemetery where Papa was buried. She cleaned off her grandfather's grave, and removed all of the sticks and twigs that had blown in during the storm. The telephone repairmen had made deep footprints in the red mud, too. They had walked right to her grandfather's grave and retrieved the broken telephone wire.

"You see, during the storm the telephone wire had blown off of the telephone pole right across her grandfather's grave. Her old dead grandfather just knew that Miss Loretta would be scared, and this was the first time he had had a chance to call her since his death and burial."

The whole store was as quiet as a church and then everyone broke into a big laugh. I know that I was listening and believing. Most of the others believed, too. Mr. Raymond Cook patted me on the head and said: "Yes, they are still making ghosts even today. Just like in the past times, most of them ghosts are ok people just trying figure out what has done happened to them and where do they go from here. Take what you want from this and do with it what you will!"

Mr. Cook got up and walked right out into night.

Well, I got up from off'n my carbide can that I had been holding onto for the last half an hour so tight that my fingers hurt and started up the road for home. It was a warm night and the stars were out. I went up over the hill past Miss Kadle's, past Mod Snider's and I rounded the turn at Sam Smith's and the Lytton Cemetery. As I started toward the stretch to the pond, I was picking up speed. By the time I got to the pond I was running like a wild Indian. I passed the pond in a flash. I did not slow down until I was at Uncle Nelson's driveway. Uncle Nelson was up at the mailbox. He said that I sounded like a horse coming around the curve. "Boy, is there a haunt or something after you?"

"I don't know, but if there is, the thing is going to have to run me down to catch me!"

Do I believe in ghosts? Well, school is still out on that question. But, still I don't see any need to take any extra chances.

I do not know if Mr. Raymond Cook made the story up on the spot or heard it told to him as a child. For all I know he read it in a book. It doesn't matter much to me these days. But I still remember how I felt when he talked and how I ran.

To my mother's dying days she insisted that she had seen Mr. Walker Snider come around the corner of the house the way he did when he was alive. In life he never came in the house, and in death he still did not come. His ghost just walked past the corner of the house. Never saw him myself. But I had no answer, and I ain't going to start to question my mother now!

Memories Are a Funny Thing

*Morrie Long once told me: "Now if it is worth anything,
it ain't going to be easy to get and it'll be even harder
to keep."*

CAN ANYONE TRULY EXPLAIN how memories work?
Just a few weeks ago, I drove through Christiansburg
and over the road into Cambria. I was puzzled by my
overflowing memories of this place.

The memory of the old mill came to mind. I bet
it was taken down 30 years ago. It once stood on the
corner at the first intersection going into town. There
is a traffic light there now. The memory of the smell of
the dry molasses is just as sweet and strong today as
it was 50 years ago. The smell of ground animal feed
dust was thick. I could almost taste it in the air! With
a little blink, I could feel mill dust in my eyes. I always
sneezed when the air was thick like fog with grinding
dust. I could see the miller standing there sacking
feed with a thick dust collection in his eyebrows and
whiskers. It was so funny I even had to sneeze.

I looked up the main street toward the liquor
store. It seems like about every time we went to the
mill we also went to the liquor store. It appeared
to me that once Daddy or Shorty had made their
purchase, it was a race to get to the railroad tracks in
Merrimack so we could have a drink of liquor. Daddy

always bought a big RC Cola. He would take a big gulp of hooch and then take a drink of the RC for a chaser, before he handed me the RC to drink. As I got bigger, Uncle Shorty or Nelson would hand me the bottle of liquor, too. I always got the leftover chaser to drink on the way home. Sometimes I think who drank at the Merrimack railroad tracks was a factor of size, not age. I was right big for my age.

Today, I stop at the Merrimack railroad tracks, too. No not to open a new bottle of bourbon, but to put my bicycle out on the walking trail. Local governmental leaders have made a linear park out of the area. There are historical markers of long-since-closed coal mines. But there is not one thing there that doesn't remind me of our trips to the mill and the liquor store.

I drove through Cambria and stopped at a nice neatly remodeled country store. I stopped at an old antique shop. I walked through the old train station that is now a toy store. But my memories made me set in the car for a few minutes and think back to a time when this old store was a place where we went for stovepipe, replacement of small farm tools, garden fertilizer, canning jars and such. The nice, newly sanded floors did unveil the giant big boards used 100 years ago in the construction. In days gone by, the roughness of the lumber was worn smooth by dirty farm shoes and mill grit. The shiny wax and the smell of potpourri were as confusing to my senses as the pretty nice ladies purchasing little ornaments for their yard and set-a-rounds for the holidays. There were no big fertilizer trucks anywhere to be seen. Time does not march on—it flat out runs!

I still can remember stopping down along the railroad tracks in that old red Chevrolet truck, the one with the loose gear-shifter. Sometimes the shifter would just bounce out of the transmission. Today, no one would have such a truck. But, in 1972, I thought it was a little cream puff. Just slow down and push the shifter back down between the shifting forks and go on.

Epilogue

A society grows great when old men plant trees whose shade they know they shall never sit in.

Greek Proverb

I HAVE THOUGHT ABOUT writing my story of American chestnut trees for a good while now. The American chestnut tree has fascinated me for many years. As a kid, I listened to Daddy and Uncle Shorty and Mr. Luther talk about an old dead tree near the garden fence. Part of Mr. Luther's house was sided with American chestnut and he always said, "Well, that part ain't going to rot." As an adult, I have walked the woods looking at old stump sprouts. As a 4-H extension agent, I joined and partnered with a major research program focusing on seed collection and the restoration of the American chestnut tree. Even with all this, I just never seemed to think I am the best writer for this job. Today, I bought a small box of chestnuts that were shipped in here from—of all places—Italy, and I started to think. Well, that could be a problem in itself.

Regularly, as a part of my job as an extension agent, I am asked to walk through the mountain to identify a chestnut tree. "This has got to be an American chestnut tree. I discovered it while squirrel hunting, and I knew you wanted to know. Look at how far we are back in the mountain," landowners tell me. I am so saddened to inform them that the big chestnut tree they are so proud of discovering is a Chinese chestnut tree. After a few minutes of looking around the site, we discover an old house foundation and often remains of fences. "Once this was an open area with a house, pastures, and a planted Chinese chestnut. Mother Nature has simply reclaimed the area," I inform the person

Believe it or not, a few weeks ago while I was visiting in Charlotte, North Carolina, for some reason my hostess got up without a word and started searching her storage cabinets. When she returned, she had a small box containing her collection of chestnut seeds. She had collected seeds from every country she visited around the world. The date and location were written on each. "They were very pretty trees, so I collected the seeds as a reminder," she explained. This, I think, is kind of the way the Chinese blight was introduced into America. People just brought seeds and seedlings from other countries. This has inspired me.

When I was a kid, every fall Uncle Shorty and Daddy would load us kids up in Uncle Shorty's old International pickup truck and haul us to Craig County. There were kids hanging out both sides of the open truck bed as we drove through the fall-colored mountain. The ride over was just like riding in a convertible without any car wrapped around you. Fun stuff!

The reason for the trip was to pick up chestnuts. There was this one man named Orvell Orange who had no less than 25 Chinese chestnut trees lining his driveway. People came from everywhere to pick up chestnuts. I would climb the trees like a big fox squirrel and shake out the nuts that were on the verge of falling. Mr. Orvell Orange would tell us about the mountains when he was child and about the old American chestnuts.

"These Chinese chestnuts nuts are big compared to the smaller American chestnut seeds," he said. "I like to eat them, but the old timey ones was much better. No sir, there is no way to compare the taste. These here Chinese chestnuts are not as good."

He would start off on long stories about old timey American chestnut trees. Most of this information I had heard from Mr. Luther and my family, but the one thing that Mr. Orange said different was this one phrase: "spring chestnut snow."

"There were so many American chestnut trees that when they flowered the mountains looked like a light snow had fallen on the tops of the trees. The smell of the flowers reached all the way to the bottom of the mountain. The odor was thick and pungent," remembered Orvell Orange. "Make you cough and sneeze," he said.

Some people said the smell was too strong. I have never seen the spring chestnut snow, or smelled the strong smell of millions of American chestnut trees in flower. I would like to have at least once. We ate hundreds of the Chinese chestnuts, carried pockets full to school and once in awhile baked them in the oven. We even planted a few out next to the driveway from Uncle Shorty's. These nuts were my only experience with chestnuts until I became an adult. Except, that is, looking at the little dead twigs near the garden.

So, I am going to tell you what I have heard, learned and think, plus some of the old stories, too. A scientist I am not; I am just a most willing participant in the long line of those following the melancholy story of the American chestnut tree! Honestly, you could take all I know on the subject and about $7.50 and purchase a good cup of coffee and a cinnamon bagel at your local Starbucks. Cinnamon bagels are my favorites, especially if you add a little cream cheese.

A onetime close friend recently told me that I could not carry a writer's pencil box. This feller ain't my friend any more either. But, I just keep plugging along.

Another thing I do not know exactly where to put is this piece of information, so I am going to add it in right here. A question that I have been asked many times over the years is: "Why haven't they found a cure for the American chestnut blight? Modern science has found cures of lots of other things."

Yes, lots of cures have been found for diseases of every description. To date and to my knowledge, no cure for the American chestnut blight has been discovered. Here is the best way of describing the problem. (I also reserve the right to be a little wrong here. As stated earlier, I am no plant pathologist and don't even get to play one on the radio.) The American chestnut tree has no natural resistance to the introduced fungus _Cryphonectria parasitica_. This is an airborne fungus moved by the wind and people. Commonly, it is referred to as a blight. So back in the early part of the century, soon after the introduction of the blight, it went through the population of American chestnuts kind of like the influenza virus did the human population. It just went wherever the wind went.

Research work has been ongoing since the early 1900s, when plant breeders, geneticists, foresters and tree scientists began efforts to understand the blight. A few scientists started trying to cross-pollinate the Chinese chestnut with the American chestnut to breed in resistance.

Another group of scientists focused on finding natural resistance in the American chestnut. This approach concentrates on cross-pollinating surviving American chestnut trees to create a line of "All American Intercross." Individuals have discovered American chestnut trees in the wild that have lived long enough to bear fruit. These trees are being cross-pollinated in an effort to build a more resistant strain.

To date, this resistant tree has not been created. I was once told that the more we start to learn about the blight, the more questions come up. It is my understanding that resistance in the American chestnut tree may be borne on six or seven recessive genes. All of these genes must act differently, in a dominant fashion and in unison. No one knows the number of cross-pollinations this will take. Another point, if the genes do perform the way scientists wish, there must be someone to know this has happened, and that could take 25 years of watching. The magical seed could already have appeared and disappeared, because a squirrel ate the nut. A forest fire might have burned the sapling or a bulldozer pushed the stump and seedling over the bank. Finding a fix for the American chestnut has been a long and drawn-out process. But a lot has been learned, too!

I think that the loss of the American chestnut tree is one of North America's worst environmental disasters—ever. Sadly, few have ever heard of this disaster. People have heard of the Exxon Valdese, the big oil well problem in the Gulf of Mexico and forest fires and droughts all over the Midwest. But not many are aware of the death of the American chestnut tree. Today, if you stop a person on the street and ask him or her about an American chestnut, most likely you'll hear: "Yes, I know about the American chestnut. We have one in our backyard, and the seed burrs get in my feet. It is hard to mow over them, too."

No, the tree they remember is a Chinese chestnut. For example, not long ago at a gathering of 17 teenagers, I passed out a picture of some very large American chestnut trees. The statement on the bottom read: "Appalachian Forest and American Chestnut 1909."

"Well, they are some big trees," I heard. No mention of the plight of these giants.

The American chestnut tree was a titan of a tree and grew in numbers that were unimaginable. I once was told that a squirrel could climb an American chestnut tree in Boston, Massachusetts, and walk from limb to limb all the way to Tupelo, Mississippi, without ever touching ground. Statements like this seem to be almost impossible, but they do serve to make a point. Before 1900, the population of American chestnut trees numbered in the billions. One estimate said as many as 3,000,000,000 while another firmly stated 10,000,000,000. I saw a caption under a picture that referred to the American chestnut as the "Redwoods of the East." Without question, they were the most dominant tree in the Appalachian deciduous forest and a valued economic resource.

Then, round about 1900, an airborne fungus, commonly referred to as the "Chestnut Blight," was introduced when Chinese chestnut trees were planted. In the entire history of the American chestnut, it had never been exposed to this fungus and therefore had no natural resistance. In contrast, the Chinese chestnut had developed alongside the fungus, and was thereby protected by some form of natural resistance. When the wind blew, the new disease rode it, and wherever the wind carried the disease the trees died.

Each year the American chestnut was a most dependable source of high-energy food, one of the main food sources for animals. The flowers filled the trees in late May and early June, after the last killing spring frost. The seeds matured very quickly through the summer, and the burrs began cracking open and dropping in October.

In the 1930s there was an Appalachian forest researcher named Lucy Brawn who came to Salt Pond Mountain. There, on the Mountain Lake Resort property, she established a hundred 1/10-acre plots. Her published data stated that more than 90 percent of the trees on that section of the mountain were American chestnut. Yes, that's nine out of ten trees.

No more.

No longer is the skyline dominated by the giant American chestnut trees. No longer can a squirrel walk from tree to tree on the limbs. No longer can the timber industry depend on American chestnut lumber. No longer are there American chestnuts roasting on open fires in the cities.

Just by chance, a few years ago, I met an older gentleman as I drove down the Blue Ridge Parkway with my convertible top down, just enjoying the warm days of late spring. He was selling old pieces of American chestnut fence-rails that he had made into flower-bud vases. These rails may have been cut around the turn of the century, but because the wood is so high in tannic acid, it is extremely resistant to rot. I bought one, just to help me remember his stories.

175

Lonnie Wright is his name. Lonnie just might be 25 or 30 years older than me. Since I am 61 that would make Lonnie, I am guessing, somewhere around 90 to 100 years old. And he looked every bit of it, too. Some of his bigger wrinkles had large wrinkles on them; he had spent at least one normal lifetime out in the sun. I think he was a retired farmer, only he didn't know that he was retired yet. We talked of the upcoming spring and his fences needing some repair. He said he needed to be working in his pastures before the brush got too far ahead of him, how a lot of rain had got the ground too wet to get the corn in. And he spoke of life as you get older. Me, I just leaned back on an old chair to listen and think of my own life and get a close-up view of what life would soon bring me.

I told him that I was trying to learn how to be retired, too, and I just did not seem to be able to get the hang of it. Lonnie said, "Getting older just seems to have a life of its own, don't it? And it moves on at its own pace, and there ain't one thing you can do about it."

During all of the talking, I purchased one of his little flower vases. In the middle of our conversation he stopped talking and looked up at me. He then asked, "You say that you used to collect chestnut seeds and plant 'em with young people?"

I chuckled and answered, "I once did."

"Well, I'll be dogged," said Lonnie Wright.

He then told me that on his farm there once were many chestnut trees, but about all that is left is a barn full of old Chestnut fence-rails. "I put them up in the loft more than 20 years ago. They had got down on the ground and were starting to rot. In fact, they ain't much good any more except for building a fire under a hog-scalding barrel and making these here little flower vases.

"The old barn on the place is built out of Chestnut lumber too. Back in the 1930s, Pap used green, just-cut chestnut lumber off'n the place as siding for the barn. All of the trees were just about dead anyways, but still sappy. Pap just had to do something with all the dead trees."

He chuckled and continued. "After a while some of the boards just fell off. The sap made the nails rust away. We had to go back and nail them to the barn a second time. That was 60 or more years ago, and they are as good as the day we put them back up. We made about everything out of chestnut lumber— cabins, furniture, crossties for the railroad and fires for kitchen stoves.

"For us, living out here in the country, them American chestnut trees were part of everyday life. In the fall of the year, all of us kids would rake up buckets full and eat them until we were sick. They were just something different to eat. We put buckets of them in the cellar and ate them most of the winter. The rest of them we fed to the hogs or milk cows. Hogs liked them more than we liked raking and picking them up.

"Them briers off'n them burrs would get in your fingers and swell up like a locust thorn, but the hogs grew big and fat on almost free feed. Daddy turned part of the milk cows dry in late summer, and the cows pastured in the shade of them big trees all the way up into the early fall. When the cows freshened, they were fat and their hides were slick; plus the calves were big and healthy because their mothers ate them chestnuts. Our family always killed a beef or two for winter. Them rascals always were as fat as town dogs, too."

The old fellow added that through the 1940s and even after the war, he could remember his daddy cutting dead, wormy chestnut logs and sending them off to the furniture factory, although at that point they were not of much value. American chestnut trees were part of his family's life, which was true of the whole Appalachian region from Maine to Georgia. The stately trees were just part of the culture.

In my real-life job as an extension agent, one of the most interesting projects I ever encountered was the American Chestnut Cooperators' Foundation. When I initiated youth involvement through my 4-H program, I found that few young adults and almost no youth even knew of the plight of the American chestnut tree. My goal was to teach the young people in the county about the loss of the American chestnut tree, teach science and offer an opportunity for them to be good stewards of the environment. Before the 1930s, the chestnut trees ranged in size from a hoe handle all the way up to a tree with a ten-foot diameter. Some reached more than one hundred feet into the sky.

I was no more than five or six years old when I first heard the words "American chestnut tree." My own personal understanding of the tree came from none other than my father and Uncle Shorty. Below Grandmother's garden, just over the fence on Mr. Luther Snider's property right near the old roadbed, grew three American chestnut trees—actually not really trees, just stump sprouts with five or more old dead snags growing out of them. To me, they looked like a clump of half living big stickweeds; not trees at all.

Every once in a while, me and Uncle Shorty would climb over the garden fence and walk over and look at the trees. I think we went more to look out at the river and make plans for fish-gigging or possibly to think about squirrel-hunting than to measure our concern over those little trees. "Aw shit, them trees are going to die too." Uncle Shorty would explain.

At the time none of this talk of trees made any sense at all. Well anyway, Daddy, Shorty and Mr. Luther would just look at the stump sprouts and shake their heads and keep walking. Like me, they had no clue as to what was killing the trees. Nor did they see the environmental ramification of the loss of this species of tree. I am sorry to say that to most of their generation the trees were little more than firewood, lumber, pockets full of chestnuts for eating and habitat for hunting. The mountains stayed green, and the importance of the American chestnut just slipped into the past.

Daddy said that in his time there never were many living American chestnut trees on River Ridge. By the early 1940s most of the chestnut trees had been cut down or were just dead trees standing with no bark. They made great firewood, because the wood was light and easy to split. But, there were a few big living ones still about.

Elmer also said, "They were some kind of big tree." They were so tall that you needed a 22-caliber rifle to hunt them. If squirrels were up in the top, a shotgun would be hard-pressed to cut it's way through all the leaves and still have enough power to kill a squirrel. Again, I wasn't there, but I have no reason not to believe what Daddy said. He was my father, and little boys always want to believe everything their father says. Today I think the American chestnut must have been one of the most important trees ever.

When I began collecting and planting seeds, older people just came out of the woodwork with stories to tell me about their memories of these magnificent trees. For example, one senior citizen told me she just could not make herself eat turkey anymore. She grew up in mountains near a livestock market. Her father, who was a butcher and sold fresh meat off the pole, had fenced off a 30- or 40-acre boundary of timber. Almost every tree was an American chestnut.

When the seeds ripened her dad killed wild turkeys every day or so for the family to eat. "Them chestnuts are for the hogs and cattle to eat, not turkeys and kids," he claimed. The older lady said, "We ate so much turkey that today I just can't make me eat it." In the fall her father would purchase all the skinny hogs and cattle he could afford. These animals were turned in on the chestnuts to fatten. When the weather turned cold and all the chestnuts were eaten, the animals were then sent to slaughter.

I have heard my own family tell that up until about 1930 lots of farmers branded or ear-notched their livestock, so everyone would know who owned each animal, and turned them loose to roam and forage in the mountains, eat up all the chestnuts and fatten for the coming winter. Your neighbor's animals just roamed with yours. Come spring, everyone got together and drove the stock out of the mountains and sorted out the animals and their offspring. American chestnuts were free animal feed, and almost all Appalachian farmers took advantage of this free feed.

Another story passed on to me spoke of people going to the mountain when the chestnuts began to fall. They would pick up and rake up sacks full of chestnuts and haul the sacks to local train stations. There, empty train cars bound for cities would be filled with chestnuts. They were used as animal feed kind of like corn is used today.

People ate the seeds, too. Think back to chestnuts roasting on an open fire. Roasted chestnuts were sold as a fall or holiday food in major cities. Before 1900, people in Appalachia also ate American chestnuts.

At work one day, I received a call from a lady who asked me if I was the "Chestnut Man." When I told her that I guess that I could be, she continued: "We have heard of you. My father lives in New York, and he is very old. He would like to help you collect seeds for a day." So we marked our calendars for a fall Saturday, met at the Mountain Lake Resort for breakfast and then headed for the seed orchard.

The old man told me that his very first paying job was carrying water to men building a new mill in their community. At the time, he was only six or seven years old, but he remembered that the men of the community went to the mountain and cut a very large tree for a ridge beam for the mill. All of the horses in the community were hitched to this big chestnut log to drag it to the construction site.

"All the horses" I found to be a funny statement.

"All"—was that 2 or 6 or 18? I still don't know, but "all the horses" were used. At the site, workers started shaping and hewing the log with axes and adzes. After a while, they had a giant piece of lumber measuring 2" by 12" by 100' long. "Why use such a giant piece of lumber," I asked. Simple—it was there and they had it and it was free. Again, I did not see the mill or the log or even the ridge beam. But the story does bespeak of the size of those gentle giants.

Today, the ancient American chestnuts trees are gone, possibly never to be seen again. In these modern times a 12" by 2" piece of lumber 100' long could only be cut from a giant redwood, or a Sequoia or possibly a large sugar pine or one of the other giant trees out west. But in 1920, the people from a small town in New Jersey just went to the woods to cut this giant ridge beam for a mill. Times do change. Me, I would like to walk though the mill. I would even like to help take down the mill. I would just like to see the ridge beam.

Over the years that I worked on this issue, many youth learned the stories, and they can remember them as well as I can. Even as the project faded, some of them who are now full-grown women and men will stop me and ask if I ever go check on their trees? I ask if they ever go see them. I am sorry to say, few ever walked back into the mountain to look at their effort, but almost all can recount the story of an airborne fungus introduced into America and how more than a billion American chestnut trees died.

So I will keep my small flower vase made from chestnut rails. I will set it up on the mantle at home and each time look at it I will think back on my collection of stories. Possibly my vase is just meant to hold funeral flowers over the lost species.

American chestnut trees were once so plentiful that miles of pasture fence were made from chestnut rails and thousands of residents sneezed from the smell of the pollen in the spring. If you drive slowly up and down the Blue Ridge Parkway, you will still see a few of these old rail fences. Fence rails were made from lots of different trees, but American chestnuts were the most popular. Why? There were millions of trees; the wood was light so newly cut rails were easy to move; the wood is high in tannic acid resistant to rot so they last a long time; and the rails are very easy to manufacture since the wood is straight-grained and very easy to split. An old man once told me, "Hammer a wedge into one end of a log, and it will split all the way to the other end."

Keep in mind, there were trees everywhere for the cutting and taking. They were once cut and hauled out of the mountain for their bark, as well. The American chestnut bark is so high in tannic acid that it was used in the tanning of leather. At one time leather was processed at the Old Tannery in Pearisburg, Virginia, not far from River Ridge. When the American chestnut bark became hard to come by, the tanning industry moved. Never know, it could have been the market or new environmental regulations.

A few years back some of my family met at a small town on the Kentucky–Ohio border. I think that this was one of the best long weekends I ever spent. I swam in the pool, ate lot of good food and played with my little niece some.

One of the funniest activities I have ever been

a part of took place this weekend. Someone had the idea that we would take a mule ride through the backwoods of the resort. Well, I did not want to go, because I am the original "Little Fat Boy," and I just might break a good size mule in half. Plus, "Kate the Mule" tried to kill me off one time long ago. So, I said, "I will just set here on this big log and wait for you all to come back."

"No way," said this man. "Heck, I have a mule as big as you are fat."

Now talk about building up the excitement.

Well, out of the barn a hostler leads a mule as big as any four-hoofed animal I have ever seen. It looked to be about half horse, about half mule and about half hippopotamus.

"This here is a full-blooded Missourah Mule, and he has carried bigger people than you."

"Are you sure? I go upwards to an eighth of a ton?"

Well, a couple of real strong-looking young boys pick me up and set me on the saddle of this gentle giant!

Off we go through the woods and, to be real honest, I was having a good time. The big mule must have walked this path a lot. He stepped over every rock and fallen tree-trunk and slid down each small hill with the greatest of ease, while I stayed in the saddle. After a little while we stopped in a wide place to take a break. I looked back into the woods a very short distance, and there stood an American chestnut tree about eight feet tall. It was growing out of a clump of 20 or so dead stump sprouts. I did not say anything. I have seen hundreds of stump sprouts just like this one.

When we got back to the barn, the two big young men held onto my hippopotamus-crossed mule, and I climbed all the way to the ground. Everyone in the group started talking about how much they liked the ride and what was the best part. I told the group, "I truly enjoyed myself and was thankful for such a fine mule. I enjoyed seeing the American chestnut tree, and maybe this one will be the one that proves to be naturally resistant."

The old man that led the group said to me, "Did you say American chestnut?"

"Why, yes sir. In Virginia I have been working with a 4-H American Chestnut Restoration Project."

The man asked me to show him the stump sprout, so we climbed back on the mules. Yes, I clambered up the side of mine this time. I told the man that I saw it at the place where we took the short break. He said he knew where I was talking about and we'd take a shortcut. We rode almost straight up the side of this steep hill. It was all I could do to keep from sliding off'n the ass of this giant big mule. Don't ask me how, but I stayed on him. Within 20 minutes, we were standing beside the tree.

"I know that I have been past this very spot more than a hundred times in the past few years, and I never even saw this tree. Are you sure that is an American chestnut?"

When I told him I was, and that I'd seen many over the years, we sat down on the clean dirt to talk, and he began: "According to my family, once this whole valley was full of American chestnut trees. My family pastured cattle and hogs in the woods. The old barn where we kept the mules my family built out of chestnut cut off the place. Then one day, they just started dying. You think this one will make it?"

I answered candidly, "No one knows, but it looks like all the other stump sprouts that died, so most likely this will tree will die in year or so."

"Well, I am going to clean up little around it, and the next time we take break, I will tell everyone to take a look at an American chestnut tree," he said. "I will tell them about how big they were."

We headed for home on the mules. When we started back down over the hill toward the barn to the place where I almost slid off the backend of the mule, I thought that other parts of me were going to get scrubbed off in a most painful way. When me and the real big mule parted ways, I said to myself. "That may very well have been my last mule ride." But, I still have a strong fondness for American chestnut trees and love for the stories!

Not too long ago, an acquaintance who was right upset with one of his neighbors said to me, "He will go through hell just a poppin."

I laughed a few times and asked, "What did you say—go through hell just a poppin?"

"Yes," he explained, "back in the old days about everyone had both a cook stove and a heat stove.

When you burnt chestnut wood, the stove just popped like popcorn. At this same time a lot of the caskets were made of American chestnut, so when that casket made its way to hell, it too started to pop."

I just like the way all aspects of American chestnut found their way into our vocabulary, and the expressions are still used today. I use those expressions every time I can work them into a conversation.

Recently, I did a little research for this story, which consisted of talking to old-timers who had truly seen the big trees. Some, like me, may have just heard their fathers tell the stories so much that they only think they saw the trees, but the stories do live on! One of the fellows said, "You have not made mention of a turkey drive. Farmers once turned small white turkeys loose in the mountains to fatten for market on fallen chestnuts. When the turkeys were fat, people went to the mountain and drove them all out of the chestnut trees to the local market."

From Longfellow's poem, "The Village Blacksmith": "Under the spreading chestnut tree the village smithy stands..." My bother Melvin, is a blacksmith of great renown. He grows American chestnut seeds for me to distribute. He is poet some, too!

28789698R00114

Made in the USA
Columbia, SC
25 October 2018